Radio Nation

Radio Nation

Communication, Popular Culture, and
Nationalism in Mexico, 1920–1950

Joy Elizabeth Hayes

The University of Arizona Press

Tucson

First printing

The University of Arizona Press

© 2000 Joy Elizabeth Hayes

All rights reserved

♾ This book is printed on acid-free, archival-quality paper.

Manufactured in the United States of America

05   04   03   02   01   00   6   5   4   3   2   1

Library of Congress Cataloging-in-Publication Data

Hayes, Joy Elizabeth
   Radio nation : communication, popular culture, and nationalism
in Mexico, 1920–1950 / Joy Elizabeth Hayes.
      p. cm.
Includes bibliographical references and index.
   ISBN 0-8165-1852-1 (acid-free paper)
   1. Radio broadcasting—Mexico—History.   2. Radio
broadcasting—Social aspects—Mexico.   3. Radio broadcasting
policy—Mexico. I. Title.
   PN1991.3.M4 H59   2000
   384.54′0972—dc21

                                      00-008113

British Library Cataloguing-in-Publication Data

A catalogue record for this book is available from the British Library.

For

Richard Wightman Fox

Teacher and Mentor

Contents

Figures

Acknowledgments

In the almost ten years that I have been working on this project I have accumulated an enormous debt to individuals and institutions alike. None of my research would have been possible without the support of the following institutions and agencies: the Department of Communication Studies, the College of Liberal Arts, and the Committee on International Travel at the University of Iowa; the Center for U.S.-Mexican Studies, the Center for Iberian and Latin American Studies, and the Department of Communication at the University of California, San Diego; the University of California Institute for Mexico and the United States; and the Spencer Foundation.

Most important, though, is the debt I owe to the people who supported me throughout this project. First, I would like to thank the helpful staff members of the Archivo Histórico de la Secretaría de Educación Pública (SEP), the Archivo General de la Nación, the U.S. National Archives, the State Historical Archives of Wisconsin, the Bancroft Library, Syracuse University Library Special Collections, the General Electric Hall of History, the Rockefeller Archive Center, and the University of Texas Benson Latin America Collection. At the Departamento de Correspondencia y Archivo of the Presidencia de La República, Lic. Ma. Leticia Morales Castellanos was exceptionally generous and supportive. Many, many thanks for the help and guidance given me.

A number of people offered helpful criticism on various drafts of the book. Many thanks to Dudley Andrew, Kathy Battles, Bruce Gronbeck, Charles Hale, Dan Hallin, Kathleen Newman, Laurie Reynolds, and several anonymous reviewers for their close readings and thoughtful observations. Inspiration, conversation, and long-term intellectual support came from Sarah Banet-Weiser, Barry Carr, Susan Davis, Dan Hallin, Harold Hinds, Robert Horwitz, Steve Luck, Corynne McSherry, the Radio Reading Group (Kathy Battles, Jay Beck, Rob Hill, and Alison McCracken), Laurie Reynolds, América Rodriguez, Ramón Eduardo Ruíz, Charles Tatum, and Eric Van Young. Essential research support was provided by Ernesto Acevedo-Muñoz, Michele Carlson, Sam Samuels, Kevin Shroth, and Shih-che Tang. For help with the preparation and publication of this manuscript I would like to thank Karla Tonella, Melinda Conner, and Patti Hartman. I especially want to thank Ernesto for his outstanding research contribution. While I greatly benefited from collaboration with these generous and hard-working souls, I alone hold responsibility for the inevitable errors and shortcomings herein.

Other kinds of much-needed support and distraction were generously offered by Miss Bear, Melissa Binder and Family, Kischka Blust, Chris Brenneman, Dori Burnham and Adrian Ortiz, Steve Duck, Dell Edwards, Kathleen Farrell, Barbara Fenton, Mya Hayes, Miles Hayes, Anita Johnson-Kraiger and Phil Kraiger, Jacqui Michel, La Familia Ordoñez, Laurie Reynolds, Lester Silvestrini, Mary Slaughter, and "Buckshot" Buchanan. I couldn't have done it without you!

Introduction

The modern nation would be inconceivable without mass communication technologies that extend cultural practices, symbols, and narratives to millions of people simultaneously across great distances. While other institutions build national unity and identity (including the central state, the education system, commercial markets, and labor unions), the role of mass communication in nation building has been both underestimated and understudied. This is particularly true in the case of Mexico, where a new mass communication technology—radio broadcasting—came to maturity at the exact moment that the state and commercial interests were looking for an economical means of reaching the Mexican people. These interests turned to radio as a tool for integrating the political, cultural, and economic lives of a largely nonliterate population. Beginning in the late 1920s, Mexico became a radio nation.

This book investigates the intersection of radio broadcasting and nation formation across three general fields of historical terrain. First, I track the history of radio development from the beginning of broadcasting through the television era.[1] With the exception of a volume by Fernando Mejía Barquera, these formative years have received scant attention from Mexican communication scholars (Mejía Barquera, 1989; Hayes, 1993a). Second, I provide a critical history of twentieth-century nation building and engage recent debates on the meaning of "the nation" and "national culture" in Mexican history (Lomnitz-Adler, 1992; Joseph and Nugent, 1994a; Rubin, 1997). Third, I explore popular culture in Mexico as an arena of political struggle and a form of cultural expression that became the primary material of both radio broadcasting and Mexican nationalism.

The relationship among popular culture, broadcasting, and nationalism in Mexico was shaped by a specific historical context: the period of nation building and cultural construction that followed the military phase of the Mexican Revolution. During this period of cultural revolution (1920–40), the Mexican state invested heavily in cultural policies and projects designed to modernize and nationalize the country's dispersed citizenry (Vaughan and Lewis, n.d.). To a large extent, the state's actions were an effort to harness and control cultural processes unleashed by the Revolution's popular uprisings and armed struggles. As populations moved and mingled in new and unfamiliar social settings, people used popular culture—music and dance, stories and humor, arts and crafts—as a primary means of communication and a tool for building community. Official cultural policies, then, reflected the state's effort to mediate between its own interests and the larger processes of cultural transformation that were beyond its control. In this environment, particularly under the activist governments of the late 1920s and 1930s, the state embraced both nationalism and radio broadcasting as ideal means of mediating and moderating the vibrant force of popular culture.

An Overview of Radio Development

Both during and after the period of cultural revolution, Mexican radio broadcasting was shaped by the clash and collaboration of various social forces, including U.S. corporate and state interests, Mexican media entrepreneurs, state institutions, and radio audiences. By the mid-1920s, government regulations were in place that gave the Mexican state significant control over the medium and institutionalized a mixed system of state and commercial broadcasting. While these regulations limited the direct role of U.S. corporations in Mexican radio, they encouraged the rise of Mexican broadcasting companies that drew heavily on North American capital, technology, and cultural conventions.

The 1930s witnessed the rapid growth and consolidation of commercial broadcasting together with a wave of government activism in the radio field. Although the period of state activism was relatively brief, it had a lasting impact on Mexican broadcasting by promoting an official version of Mexican musical culture over both government and commercial broadcasting stations. The fact that radio audiences reacted positively to commercialized versions of "typical" Mexican songs encouraged broadcasters to comply with the state's nationalistic broadcasting policies. By the early 1940s Mexico had half a dozen radio networks and a highly organized and coordinated broadcasting industry. At the hub of the radio industry stood Emilio Azcárraga Vidaurreta, a radio entrepreneur who controlled Mexico's most powerful radio station, XEW, and operated the nation's two most extensive networks. Azcárraga's position of power increased during World War II as his organization became the primary outlet for U.S. propaganda programming and advertising dollars.

The postwar history of broadcasting, including both the rise of television and the transformation of radio, was highly constrained by the pattern of relations established in radio before and during the war. By the end of the war, the Azcárraga organization was poised to dominate television and to continue to produce a distinctly Mexican, and pro-government, programming content for the new medium. Although competition from television networks and cable companies increased in the 1990s, economic barriers to entry continued to protect Televisa's dominant position. While radio also remained a highly centralized industry, growth and specialization in the radio field produced a contradictory development of increasingly standardized modes of expression and more and more fragmented audiences.

Radio in the Context of Mexican Cultural Production

Many aspects of this historical profile will look familiar to those who study other modes of cultural production in Mexico such as cinema, the press, theater, or the recording industry. Many of Mexico's central cultural media were formed during the 1920–40 period of cultural revolution and nation building. My claim is not that radio played a more central role in nation building than other cultural media but that radio has played a unique and important part in articulating "the national" that deserves closer investigation and theorization than it has yet received. Radio broadcasting has its own institutional history, forms of representation, and modes of reception that must be examined in order to understand its cultural influence. At the same time, however, broadcasting has a long history of poaching on other cultural forms. Thus, it is helpful to examine briefly radio's debt to, and broader relationship with, other media of cultural production in Mexico.[2]

One of the most important cultural forms shaping radio broadcasting was Mexico's urban musical theater. Although it initially focused on the Spanish *zarzuela* (comic operetta) and imported both music and actors from Spain, by 1907 the theater was firmly in the hands of Mexican performers and featured national cultural themes. Beginning in the 1920s, as regional music, oral cultures, and literary traditions blended and mixed in the urban environment, the *teatro de revista* (musical review theater) emerged with a new, commercialized form of popular music as its centerpiece. As radio broadcasters (along with the recording industry) began to draw on these performers, they also admitted the theatricality, melodrama, and sentimentalism of the urban theater into radio's program forms. In particular, the musical variety format, so central to Mexican radio, reproduced the musical theater's combination of comedy sketches and musical performances (Culturas Populares, 1984; Moreno Rivas, 1989; Paranaguá, 1995).

Radio also borrowed extensively from a very different cultural medium: the urban press. Despite the difficulties of publishing in a turbulent political environment, the 1910s and 1920s witnessed a proliferation of daily newspapers in Mexico City and other urban locales. Newspapers were early investors in radio broadcasting, viewing the new medium as a potential competitor to be shaped in their image and controlled if possible. While radio imported many of the representational forms of the press—from news reporting to serial fiction, advice columns, and society features—it also adopted the self-conscious "publicness" of newspaper discourse. For example, radio broadcasters solicited public responses (phone calls, letters, and telegrams) in the same way that newspapers did. Radio also incorporated the periodic quality and serial "flow" of newspaper content, providing new installments of information and entertainment on a weekly, daily, and even hourly basis (Arredondo Ramírez and Sánchez Ruíz, 1986; Mejía Barquera, 1989).

Radio's relationship with cinema, particularly sound cinema (beginning in 1931), was less a relationship of poaching than of mutual collaboration. Broadcasting and film were linked through sound technology and industrial relations that circulated narratives, popular music, and performing artists across the two media. With the construction of the Churubusco Studios under the direction of Emilio Azcárraga in 1944, the industrial ties between cinema, radio, and (soon) television were further solidified. Both cinema and radio were technologically dependent on U.S. industries and were forced to "nationalize" and adapt North American industrial practices to fit the Mexican commercial culture. All of this was done under the watchful eye of the Mexican state, which viewed both media as ideal instruments for articulating a national mythology (Ramirez Berg, 1992; Pérez Montfort, 1994; Monsiváis, 1995; Paranaguá, 1995).

As a commercial broadcasting medium, radio combined and incorporated a range of cultural practices embracing the theatricality of the stage, the public mission of the press, and the national mythology of the cinema. In its capacity as a medium of government broadcasting, radio played a different kind of role as a direct outlet for state-sponsored projects of art, culture, and education. Like the murals the government commissioned to adorn public buildings, state-operated radio stations sponsored concerts, lectures, and other cultural events designed to publicize the state's version of national history and culture. Because broadcasting combined so many different modes of cultural production, an investigation of radio history augments our understanding of cultural production in Mexico. By situating cultural practices within larger social webs of economic, political, cultural, and institutional relations, this particular broadcasting history brings a materialist perspective to the field of Mexican cultural studies.

Chapter 1 uses the example of World War II propaganda broadcasting to introduce the relationship between radio and nation in Mexican history. This example also indicates important ways in which our definitions of *radio* and *nation* can be and need to be enriched and expanded. For example, the case of World War II broadcasting shows how the nation can be understood as a set of dominant social practices that nevertheless face resistance from both outside and inside the national space. Finally, this chapter uses a media history perspective to contribute to recent debates over the meaning of "the national" in Mexican historiography.

Chapter 2 provides a theoretical perspective on the intertwined trajectories of radio and nation. I argue that both radio and nation are antimodern social formations that actively resist the concept of modernity—the idea that human social relations are (and should be) becoming increasingly abstract, individualized, and future directed. An analysis of recent scholarship emphasizing the role of mass communication in nation building reveals the antimodern ethos of the national rituals and representations that became part of the daily experience of millions via modern communication media. This chapter also explores the antimodern dimensions of radio broadcasting; in particular, its capacity to collapse space and time, simulate corporeal contact, and create a virtual common space coterminous with the nation.

Chapter 3 frames the development of Mexican broadcasting between 1920 and 1935 within the larger historical context of U.S. expansionism, the rise of mass advertising, and post-revolutionary state building. Radio broadcasting came to maturity in Mexico at the same time that the post-revolutionary state achieved its modern institutional structure. As a consequence, the state took considerable interest in radio as a uniquely powerful tool for building political order and cultural integration. The Mexican state consciously used radio to extend its influence into civil society and in the process developed a hegemonic discourse of "national culture" to justify its growing presence in the civil sphere. At the same time, media entrepreneurs developed commercial radio stations and network systems in order to build consumer markets on a national scale.

Chapter 4 investigates one government broadcasting station—station XFX[3] operated by the Ministry of Public Education—in order to trace the state's use of radio to formulate and disseminate an official Mexican musical culture. This chapter evaluates the intentions and implications of the state's musical nationalism by examining the production and reception of XFX programming. Reports by education inspectors provide insight into rural villagers' reactions to XFX programs, and to radio broadcasting more generally. Although station XFX ultimately could not compete with commercial broadcasters for listeners, such early government radio projects provided models of nationalistic radio content that influenced Mexico's commercial broadcasters to develop their own distinctly Mexican style of radio programming.

Chapter 5 examines the forces shaping national radio content between 1935 and 1950, with a focus on the Mexico City broadcasting elite. Although Azcárraga and other Mexico City broadcasters worked to promote Mexican performers, musicians, and popular cultural forms, they also served as agents for transnational media systems that took for granted the standards, styles, and formats of North American commercial radio. Under pressure from the activist administration of President Lázaro Cárdenas (1934–40), the Azcárraga Group built a strongly nationalistic radio content and positioned itself as a virtual cultural branch of the Mexican state. By the end of the 1930s this relationship was firmly in place as the government willingly turned broadcasting over to private interests, so long as those interests protected the political hegemony of the ruling party.

Chapter 6 examines presidential radio broadcasts as media events that attempted to evoke the nation through a single, paternal voice. By examining both the production and reception of presidential discourse (as evidenced in presidential speeches, press reports, and public reaction letters and telegrams), I explore the ways that national community was represented in both presidential speeches and public responses to them. This chapter follows the transformation of presidential radio discourse from the progressive and highly nationalistic Cárdenas administration to the more conservative and development-oriented regime of his successors, Manuel Ávila Camacho (1940–46) and Miguel Alemán (1946–52).

Chapter 7 investigates the impact of World War II on radio broadcasting in Mexico, focusing on the activities of the U.S. Office of the Coordinator of Inter-American Affairs (CIAA). This government agency used the discourse of Pan-Americanism—the call for hemispheric unity against the Axis powers—to justify a massive advertising campaign for North American consumer culture and politics throughout Latin America. In Mexico, however, this propaganda campaign had the unexpected effect of strengthening the nationalistic radio content promoted by the Azcárraga broadcasting organization. Despite Azcárraga's hegemony over the cultural content of Mexican broadcasting, however, this control (and the content it shaped) remained deeply dependent on North American technology, industry standards, and advertising resources.

Finally, the Conclusion discusses the postwar legacy of radio broadcasting in Mexico. I argue that the development of radio broadcasting during the 1930s and 1940s fundamentally shaped the history of Mexican television. In particular, I argue that key structural aspects of television broadcasting were in place by the early postwar period—well before television itself became established. In the 1960s and 1970s the growth of television forced radio to transform itself into a new kind of medium that would complement, rather than continue, the broadcasting forms and contents that were migrating to television. Although radio became a secondary medium in the postwar period, it laid the groundwork for television's role as a primary medium for the production and reproduction of nationalist discourse. At the end of the twentieth century, television continued radio's legacy in Mexico: the country remained a radio nation.

Radio Nation

Radio, Nation, and Mexican History

During the Second World War, the U.S. government and commercial networks disseminated thousands of hours of radio propaganda in Mexico and throughout Latin America. These broadcasts of news, commentary, drama, and music celebrated "the North American way of life of individual freedom, high personal security, and a high standard of material living" (K. W. Smith, 1972:226). They suggested that by supporting U.S. policies in the region and backing the Allied war effort, Latin Americans could look forward to significant economic rewards at the war's end.

This propaganda project was orchestrated by the Radio Division of the U.S. Office of the Coordinator of Inter-American Affairs (CIAA),[1] a government agency created by President Franklin D. Roosevelt after the outbreak of war in Europe. The CIAA was staffed by volunteers from private industry who worked to promote the strategic and commercial interests of the United States in Latin America. It was directed by Nelson A. Rockefeller, who had long-standing interests in the region through his Standard Oil holdings. Donald "Don" Francisco, a "West Coast ace among advertising men" and president of the Lord and Thomas Advertising Agency, coordinated the Radio Division from Washington, D.C. (CIAA, 1942a).

In Mexico, the CIAA organized local committees of U.S. citizens to coordinate propaganda activities and enlist locally active North American corporations and advertising agencies in the undertaking. The Radio Division of the Mexican committee was headed by Herbert Cerwin, a West Coast public relations specialist who grew up in Guatemala and spoke fluent Spanish. Cerwin worked to place CIAA radio programs (produced both locally and in the United States) on Mexico's most popular radio stations. From the center of operations in Mexico City, Cerwin reported to Nelson Rockefeller that "throughout the day on an average of every fifteen minutes to a half hour, some slogan or mention is made that has definite bearing on our Allied victory or against the Axis" (Cerwin, 1942:3). By late 1945 the CIAA was reported to be "the chief time user and revenue producer for Latin American broadcasters" (Josephs, 1945a:19; Fejes, 1986:159).

Although the ubiquitous presence of CIAA propaganda on the Mexican airwaves would seem to suggest the permeability of Mexican radio—and the Mexican nation—to North American interests, CIAA operatives worried about the popularity of their broadcasts relative to other available programs. To measure the audience, they organized radio listener surveys of Mexico City and major provincial cities during the spring and summer of 1943, using a North American subsidiary, the Grant Advertising Agency, to conduct the surveys and "front" CIAA activities. In telephone interviews, CIAA workers simply identified themselves as "the Office of Radio Statistics" (Cerwin, 1943).

As part of their cloak-and-dagger strategy in Mexico, CIAA committee members developed a unique survey technique, called the "portable radio method," which allowed CIAA workers to canvas the neighborhoods of the Federal District and other cities in relative secrecy. The portable radio method required a group of young men with portable radios and flashlights to walk through neighborhoods in the evening hours and tune in the same radio programs that they heard coming from the open windows of each home (Figure 1.1). By recording the time of day and the broadcast frequency of each station they heard, surveyors were able to estimate program ratings. The survey offers a glimpse of the dynamic everyday practices that mediated radio as a cultural force. A brief overview of the CIAA survey findings reveals the contours of these power relations.

The survey report for Guadalajara describes the rich texture of radio listening habits in a provincial city. The surveyors found that during the time of the survey (April 29 to May 12), "the heat obliged the inhabitants to take their chairs to the sidewalks from the house at twilight refreshing themselves with the evening breeze and chatting to the neighbors. Naturally all

Figure 1.1 A CIAA survey worker using the "portable radio" method. (Photo by Andrée Vilas; CIAA Central Files, box 346, folder "Surveys," April 14, 1943, RG 229, U.S. National Archives, College Park, Md.)

windows and doors were left open, thus making it very easy to listen to the radios turned on in the houses. Frequently the radios would be tuned in to the Mexico City stations until late into the night since late hours make for better reception" (CIAA, 1943d:1). The powerful Mexico City stations had a significant presence in all of the provincial cities. In particular, Azcárraga's crown jewel, station XEW, dominated the Central Valley. Survey findings indicate that XEW controlled 75 percent of the Puebla market and was the most popular station in Morelia (with more than 30 percent of the market) and Guadalajara (more than 20 percent of the market). Station XEW ranked second and third in San Luis Potosí and Chihuahua, respectively; only in Monterrey and Torreón was the influence of XEW eclipsed by local stations (CIAA, 1943d).

Despite the strong position of XEW in the national radio market, the survey found that local markets nevertheless remained distinctive. Guadalajara, for example, had an unusually active radio market with ten local stations competing with station XEW for listeners. Puebla, in contrast, had only three local stations. Guadalajara stations also reflected a unique local and regional style of musical programming. *La Hora del Recuerdo (The Hour of Memories)*, for example, "composed of old-fashioned music such as waltzes, polkas, two-step, etc.," enjoyed "great popularity" (CIAA, 1943d:4). According to the survey, the preference for musical "oldies" clearly distinguished Guadalajara from other Mexican radio markets.

Along with program preferences, the survey also indicates that access to radios, and thus the size of the radio market, varied widely in different regions of the country. Assuming approximately six listeners for every radio receiver, more than 90 percent of the populations of Monterrey and Torreón had regular access to radios, compared with 79 percent in Guadalajara, 68 percent in Mexico City, and only 33 percent in Puebla and Morelia. Access to radios also varied considerably within cities, as the case of Morelia suggests: "In the outskirts of the city there are extremely poor sections whose inhabitants do not have electricity and therefore do not possess radios. In the main section of the city families own radios which although old are powerful sets, most of them being of the first RCA luxury models" (CIAA, 1943d:1). Poverty and lack of electricity limited radio reception both in rural areas and in the poorer parts of urban areas.[2] Despite radio's capacity to connect all Mexicans to a centralized, Mexico City–based broadcasting system, differences in local and regional conditions ensured that radio would not be experienced identically across the nation.

The survey also reveals something of the dynamic local contexts—often neighborhood contexts—in which radio listening took place. For example, in some areas of cities like Puebla and San Luis Potosí where electrical power for each home was limited to sixty watts, people discovered that using a fifteen-watt light bulb allowed them enough power for a radio receiver as well. This strategy indicates a degree of collective interest and ingenuity in listening to the radio despite limited resources. It also suggests a willingness to skimp on electric light in order to enjoy the radio (CIAA, 1943d).

The CIAA survey shows that radio listening was embedded in a set of social relations that shaped the way radio was experienced by groups and individuals. The custom of chatting and visiting with family, relatives, neighbors, and friends shaped the context in which radio was listened to and used as a form of entertainment and a means of information. As Jesús Martín-Barbero and others have argued, the meaning of mass media messages can be interpreted only in the context of local "mediations"—that is, local traditions, habits, and practices of interpretation and communication (Martín-Barbero, 1993a). At the same time, however, mass media such as radio fundamentally alter local contexts by linking them to larger regional, national, and international spheres of culture, politics, and economic exchange.

Using Radio to Rethink the Nation

By approaching Mexican history through the history of radio broadcasting, I propose a number of strategies for rethinking the meaning of the nation in that history. First, an understanding of radio's dual position—that is, as a technology largely controlled by transnational corporations and as a medium of Mexican national culture—suggests the need to approach the nation as a cultural sphere that is itself permeated by foreign interests and shaped by transnational relations of power. Despite the propensity of nationalists to proclaim the singularity and autonomy of their own nations, the nation as a form of social organization is the product of a modern global web of cultural, political, and economic relations. This international system informs the nation's most fundamental practices and institutions. In a more conspiratorial tone, it is often difficult to distinguish the "antination" from the nation (Cardoso, 1972).

Second, despite their centralized production, radio messages are always subject to local interpretations. An understanding of radio broadcasting as both highly centralized and highly diffuse suggests a strategy for conceptualizing the nation as both a dominant social category and a permeable reality. Although different national interests attempt to project a unitary value system and deny cultural pluralism within the national space, the everyday experience of this national culture remains radically local and subject to disruption by local "mediations."

Third, the nature of broadcast communication helps illustrate the nation as a social process or practice rather than a finished product. Radio's ephemeral character and constant flow, which require serial repetition and reenactment to make meaning, provide a model for the way that active social interests must constantly reassert the nation as the dominant social framework in the face of the social "flow" of alternative sources of social identity and allegiance. This suggests that rather than being viewed as a historical actor or agent, the nation is better understood as a historical process through which dominant social interests attempt to assert preferred models of politics and culture (Anderson, 1991; Chatterjee, 1993b). As such, the nation "registers difference even as it claims a unitary or unifying identity" (Duara, 1995:7). To understand the nation, then, one must investigate both its hegemonic construction and the cultural heterogeneity that "arises in spaces of hegemony" and continues to exist within the nation (Lomnitz-Adler, 1992:4).

Historical Debates

This study of Mexican radio history also brings a new perspective to recent debates in Mexican historical studies. In the late 1990s, Mexican historiography was characterized by a reaction to a long period of revisionist scholarship. Revisionist historians, responding in part to the regime crisis of 1968, attempted to discredit official claims that the Revolution was a popular movement by uncovering a powerful state that manipulated the masses from above. Working under the relatively strong Mexican state of the 1970s and early 1980s, revisionist scholars projected a strong state model on the past (Joseph and Nugent, 1994b; Vaughan, 1997), often employing a "transmission model" of culture that equated national culture with state ideology. In this model, official beliefs were directly "transmitted" to the masses, who (falsely) identified their interests with those of the state. At the same time, in a very different response to the perceived power of the state, the revisionist era also witnessed the explosive development of regional history as a means of bypassing the monolithic central state and studying a more integrated body of cultural and social relations.[3]

Around the time of the 1990 Meeting of Mexican and North American Historians, the regionalist movement began to coalesce with increasingly pointed critiques of the revisionist approach. Along with regionalist pioneer Eric Van Young, the conference featured Alan Knight's watershed post-revisionist paper, "Cardenismo: Juggernaut or Jalopy?" In it Knight questioned the revisionist view of the state under Lázaro Cárdenas (1934–1940) as a monolithic and overpowering "juggernaut" in Mexican political culture. He pointed to the nonstate actors and groups that challenged Cardenismo and portrayed the state, instead, as a slow and wobbly "jalopy." Knight's sharp critique dovetailed with the increasingly heavy output of regional histories that emphasized popular political action and deemphasized the role of the state (Knight, 1990, 1994a). By the mid-1990s, several important "post-revisionist" or "neopopulist" works had reached publication (Lomnitz-Adler, 1992; Van Young, 1992; Beezley, Martin, and French, 1994; Joseph and Nugent, 1994a; Knight, 1994b). In a regionalist mode, this new approach focused on decentralized, quotidian cultural practices. The transmission model of culture was largely replaced by a notion of cultural negotiation between the central state and local actors (Joseph and Nugent, 1994b; Vaughan, 1997). While Gilbert Joseph and Daniel Nugent continued to emphasize the hegemonic power of the state to shape consciousness—as did others who studied state-sponsored cultural projects and institutions (Frischmann, 1994; Loyo, 1994; Vaughan, 1997)—many neopopulists began to probe what Van Young defined as "local knowledge"; that is, "the contingent, historical, and even personalized understandings that groups of people and communities bring to ideas and cultural complexes shared in a general way with other groups" (Van Young, 1994:344). While this perspective acknowledged the importance of translocal cultural formations, it emphasized the local as the site of study.

An important reformulation of the post-revisionist perspective came in 1996 with the publication of Jeffrey Rubin's paper "Decentering the Regime" and the subsequent book with the same title (Rubin, 1997). In the article, Rubin rejected the nation altogether as a category of analysis and focused instead on "the regime, region, culture and daily life" (Rubin, 1996:90). Working from his research on Juchitán, Oaxaca, Rubin argued that in certain Mexican municipalities, "local life exhibited qualities of intensity, self-awareness, and self-definition at odds with the notion of a territory penetrated by state-centered ideological, economic, and mobilization mechanisms" (Rubin, 1996:113). Interestingly, this position rearticulated the revisionist model of national culture as state ideology. Along with discounting the structural components of state hegemony, Rubin emphasized the radical localism of politics: "Situations of contestation do not occur nationally, throughout all of Mexico, but in particular towns or regions, in particular cultural or economic arenas" (Rubin, 1996:98).

Rubin also stressed the extent to which older power structures of *caciquismo* (personal rule by a single boss) shaped local and regional politics and, in many cases, buffered and moderated the influence of the central state in local life. This theme became the focus of a 1998 Latin American Studies Association panel on Cardenismo. Papers by Alan Knight, Adolfo Gilly, and Adrian Bantjes joined Rubin's post-revisionist drive to deconstruct the central state by examining the extent to which Cárdenas worked through regional and local *cacique* (political boss) networks rather than through formal state mechanisms and political institutions. While the webs of caciquismo remained strong (although they were sometimes masked by the mass organizations and corporatist institutions promoted by Cárdenas), Knight argued that some centralized state structures did take hold and, ultimately, had a significant impact on Mexican politics and culture (Knight, 1998). My argument is that the state's structural relationship with radio broadcasting—developed under the Calles and Cárdenas administrations—was just such an innovation with long-term political and cultural consequences.

In many ways, recent "decentering" work by Rubin and others provides an important corrective to long-standing tendencies to essentialize the nation and national actors in Mexican history. It offers a helpful caution against the top-down national history that has been a helpmate to state- and nation-building projects for at least the last century and a half (Hobsbawm and Ranger, 1983; Duara, 1995). The neopopulist approach also helps to correct the transmission model of culture. For example, Claudio Lomnitz-Adler criticizes scholars for taking "methodological shortcuts—analyses of state rituals and myths, for example—that seem to lead directly to national culture without explicitly confronting the national space" (Lomnitz-Adler, 1992:5). Local meanings and experiences of culture and politics cannot be inferred from an analysis of centralized, often state-sponsored, forms of "national culture."

However, the strengths of the neopopulist approach are also its weaknesses. By focusing exclusively on the local context, these historians neglect the larger political-economic and social institutions that condition and shape quotidian practices. Neopopulists, one critic has observed, are in danger of disaggregating Mexican history "into so many regional and local bits that the relation of these to what were also national processes is overlooked" (Farmer, 1996:1135). Rather than giving up the nation as a site of historical inquiry (as Rubin did), Knight argued that historical analysis is needed at a number of different social levels, including the global, national, regional, and local, in order to provide a "thick history" of the Mexican experience (Knight, 1994c). To interpret the 1994 Zapatista uprising, for example, one must look at both the local sites of struggle and the national and international contexts within which the movement positioned itself (and was positioned)—principally by means of the mass media. Narratives, representations, and conflicts circulate across and between different regions and social arenas under the organizing institutions of national media. In this sense, social contestation *does* occur nationally (and globally) via the media of radio, film, television, and the Internet.

Although historians rarely mention mass communication, Mexican cultural critics have not neglected the media's historical role in articulating a hegemonic "Mexicanness" over and across regional and local difference. Carlos Monsiváis, for example, argues that "what movies and radio fostered and cultivated culminates with television: a national convergence of popular tastes, nonacademic information banks, a shared sense of humor, the adoption of Americanized culture, the incorporation (at different levels) of international perspectives" (Monsiváis, 1992:250). Other cultural critics have also noted the centralizing and nation-building role of the media in Mexico and Latin America more broadly (García Canclini, 1993; Martín-Barbero, 1993b; Pérez Montfort, 1994). Indeed, the critical role that the mass media play in supporting and promoting Mexico's single-party state has become a matter of increasingly frequent and open debate. The minimal coverage allotted to the burgeoning opposition parties during the 1988 and 1994 presidential elections, for example, made Televisa's special relationship to the Mexican state readily apparent (Hallin, 1994).

Mexican historiographic debates are helpful in reminding media historians that the question of radio's ability to "nationalize" Mexicans is ultimately an empirical question—and, as such, a *local* question. Although this book relies largely on traditional, centralized sources of historical documentation (such as national archives), it attempts to provide an empirical investigation of quotidian practices within the framework of social-structural analysis. Thus, national and transnational (U.S.) historical sources are used both to chart the political economy and organizational structure of the Mexican radio system and to document and interpret the local experiences of radio listeners. The strength of this approach is its ability to use radio history to investigate the construction of Mexican national culture across the different levels of global, national, regional, and local practice. Although this radio history emphasizes global and national analysis, I hope it suggests a path that others might take to bring media history to bear on the broader field of Mexican history.

The Antimodern Trajectories of Radio and Nation

Before embarking on a history of Mexican broadcasting, it is important to have a theoretical grounding for radio and nation as social practices. Indeed, a theoretical framework helps to clarify how radio is linked to the nation through both its technology and cultural form. Both radio and nation are social practices that actively resist the concept of modernity; that is, they oppose the idea that human social relations are (and should be) becoming increasingly abstract, individualized, and future-directed. At the heart of two of the most pervasive modern institutions lie profoundly antimodern politics and aesthetics.

The Nation

It is difficult to think of a more central feature of the modern social and political landscape than the nation. Modernist concepts such as "development," "progress," and "modernization" are unintelligible outside the context of a competitive, worldwide system of nation-states. At the same time, however, the literature on nationalism emphasizes the "antimodern" orientation of nation-building projects and nationalist movements. I take the term *antimodern* from T. J. Jackson Lears, who uses it to describe a nineteenth-century bourgeois intellectual and social movement that sought alternatives to the "apparent unreality of modern existence" (Lears, 1981: 5).[1] In seeking to combat this sense of instability and unreality, intellectuals and activists turned to premodern models of authority, transcendence, and "authenticity" found in archaic ideals of martial valor and in cultural practices such as mysticism and medieval arts and crafts. These "antimoderns" did not reject modernity altogether but rather assumed what Lears describes as an "ambivalent" position toward it: they continued to accept modern notions of progress and civilization even as they protested against the effects of modernity. Borrowing from Lears, then, I use the term *antimodern* to describe an ambivalent perspective toward modernity as a concept of forward-moving social change. More specifically, in the case of the nation, I use the term to characterize modern movements of national unity and integration that draw directly on premodern ideals of allegiance and authority. A number of recent nationalism studies examine how such ideals are articulated in and through nationalist discourse.

Benedict Anderson, E. J. Hobsbawm, and Terence Ranger have been especially influential in arguing that the disruptive forces of modernity—capitalism, colonialism, the representative state, new technologies—made the form of the nation possible and, at the same time, inspired the antimodern discourses at the heart of nationalism. Anderson maintains that as an "imagined political community" the nation has more affinities with the premodern practices of kinship and religion than with self-consciously held political ideologies (Anderson, 1991). In a similar vein, Hobsbawm and Ranger offer the concept of "invented traditions" to characterize the public rites and rituals of nationalism. Invented traditions are central to the backward-looking politics of nationalism in that they establish continuity with a "suitable historical past" that legitimizes social authority and grounds the nation in primordial bonds of kinship and community (Hobsbawm and Ranger, 1983). Although nationalism has a progressive component of movement toward a brilliant national future, this future is always positioned as the realization of a national destiny rooted in an ancient past, a past that promised an antidote for the change and instability represented by modernity.

According to Anderson, the emphasis on order and stability at the heart of nationalism can, in part, be traced to the origins of nationalism in the Creole-led independence movements that swept the Americas in the late eighteenth and early nineteenth centuries. Although not the earliest example, the case of Mexico clearly illustrates the conservative orientation of Creole patriotism in the face of social conflict and popular rebellion.

David Brading argues that colonial elites faced with a popular uprising of economically and socially oppressed mestizos, mulattos, and Indians developed a highly conservative language of religious and historical patriotism (Brading, 1985). This discourse aimed to evoke Mexican unity and defuse the social and racial conflict between Padre Hidalgo's insurgents and the landed Creole elite. In this context, invented national traditions ritualized the values of order and hierarchy through such figures as majestic Aztec rulers and the pious Virgin of Guadalupe.

George Mosse identifies a similar emphasis on order and hierarchy in France's populist bourgeois revolution. Along with the radical practices of popular sovereignty and representative government, the French Revolution inaugurated a new "dramatized politics" of public festivals, myths, and symbols that enacted a secular religion of the nation-state. Despite the participatory form of the national mystique, Mosse argues that this dramatized politics was fundamentally conservative. Invented national myths and symbols "were meant to make the world whole again and to restore a sense of community to the fragmented nation." Newly institutionalized and standardized folk practices enacted a national Eden that "stood outside the present flow of history" (Mosse, 1991:6). This premodern, pastoral world of happy and fecund peasants symbolized the harmony and order of the national community.

Heterosexual passion and reproduction provided another potent metaphor for national unity and order. Doris Sommer has investigated nineteenth-century Latin American romance novels as allegories for national consummation and conciliation. Focusing on novels such as *Amalia, Martín Rivas, María,* and *Enriquillo,* among many others, Sommer describes the national romance as "invariably about desire in young chaste heroes for equally young and chaste heroines, the nation's hope for productive unions" (Sommer, 1991:24). By the early twentieth century, these novels had become icons of national literature and required reading for schoolchildren. Mosse argues that the qualities of male virility, purity, and wholesomeness provided a "metaphor of the genuine, pre-industrial past, so important in legitimizing nationalism as an immutable force" (Mosse, 1985:119). At the same time, representations of feminine chastity, beauty, and modesty aimed to establish order and align the nation with a primordial past and a transcendent future (Mosse, 1985; Westbrook, 1990; De Grazia,

1992). The female body as both symbol and vessel (through procreation and reproduction) of the "authentic" national body—often represented through such icons as Marianne, Germania, or the Virgin of Guadalupe—played a central role in national narratives and traditions (Mosse, 1985; Anthias and Yuval-Davis, 1989; White, 1990; Bederman, 1995).

Finally, the antimodern trajectory of the nation becomes particularly clear in the case of postcolonial and diasporic nationalisms. Works by Partha Chatterjee on Indian nationalism and Wilson Jeremiah Moses on black nationalism provide important frameworks for conceptualizing the central tension between the values of progress or "civilization" and the search for "authenticity" in national identity and culture. For late-nineteenth- and early-twentieth-century nationalists, civilization represented the ideals of art, beauty, and knowledge embodied in Western culture. Civilization stood as both the cultural and the material ends toward which nationalists aspired to progress (Chatterjee, 1993b; Heller, 1994). Authenticity, on the other hand, captured the sense of cultural autonomy and meaningful identity that bourgeois intellectuals attributed to their countries' traditional indigenous cultures (Sommer, 1991; Tomlinson, 1992; Chatterjee, 1993a).

For these nationalists, the goal of civilization was frequently in conflict with the goal of authenticity. Although postcolonial nationalists viewed the developing West as the model for their nations' cultural and material evolution, they looked to explicitly non-Western cultural practices as the source of collective identity and national authenticity. Ultimately, the very autonomy of the national community became tied to an ethnic heritage that was viewed by Western civilization as "barbarous" or "backward." Thus, there was a fundamental conflict between the premodern, ethnic basis of national identity and the aspiration toward progress and civilization. In part, the discourse of ethnic or racial authenticity articulated by postcolonial and diasporic nationalist movements was inherited from European racialist thought (Moses, 1988; Gilroy, 1990). However, the celebration of ethnic authenticity was also an effort to assert an autonomous identity under conditions of European colonialism and domination.

In sum, nationalist discourse was forced to bridge the divide between tradition and progress, past and future. Although the nation assumed a distinctly antimodern politics and aesthetics, it was still fundamentally tied to the modern forces of capitalist production, colonial expansion, and bureaucratic organization under which it developed and spread. In particular, the modern form of the nation has been described as a "mass-mediated" form, reliant on modern technologies of mass communication for its particular structure and content. A closer look at the connection between nation and communication is necessary, then, to explain the nation's antimodern trajectory.

Nationalism and Communication

Interest in the role of communication technologies in the formation and promotion of nationalism goes back to the work carried out by Karl Deutsch in the 1950s and 1960s. Deutsch argued then that national identification was a product of social communication, and that it would intensify or weaken depending on the extent and intensity of communication practices (Deutsch 1967; Breuilly 1982). More recently Anderson renewed interest in this question with a groundbreaking analysis of print technology and nation formation. Along with Anderson, several other nationalism scholars have observed that the peculiar structure or style of nationalism is a "mass-mediated style" and that the production of national communities would be inconceivable without the technical means to extend vernacular communications to millions of people across great distances (Martín-Barbero, 1988; Hobsbawm, 1990; Tomlinson, 1992).

Anderson's examination of the role of print communication in the rise of nationalist discourse articulates some of the basic ways that communication technologies organize and shape nationalism. Focusing on the rise of nationalism among eighteenth- and nineteenth-century political elites, Anderson argues that the mass production and mass circulation of printed material (especially books and newspapers) laid the basis for national community by creating a unified field of exchange and communication among literate elites, giving a new uniformity to one vernacular language or dialect, and creating a simultaneity of experience among a dispersed population. Anderson describes these print vernaculars as "languages of power" because of their ability to push aside other, less influential, dialects and position themselves as unitary national languages (Hobsbawm, 1990; Anderson 1991).

Anderson's analysis of print capitalism draws primarily on Walter Benjamin's concept of a reconfigured sense of time and space brought on by the mechanical reproduction of language and other cultural forms through new capitalist relations of production. Anderson argues that the coming together of print technology and capitalist forms of production gave print communication its unifying capabilities and positioned it to create a sense of simultaneity on the part of a dispersed body of readers. Simultaneity— the awareness of parallel actors acting at the same time along a secular and forward-moving time line—was the product of mass-produced vernacular texts that were spread over a wide region by capitalism's "relentless search for markets." As these texts were read and experienced in (unstable, modern) social contexts in which unitary systems of religion and politics no longer held complete sway, they provided the communicative space for a new kind of "imagined" community among literate elites (Anderson, 1991). Specifically, Anderson suggests that the flow of printed material and communiqués through the bureaucratic channels of modern colonial governments mapped this new form of community onto precisely the same terrain covered by the administrative state.

Several nationalism scholars have emphasized the ability of communication technologies to make the imagined community of the nation part of the daily experience of individuals and social groups. Focusing on nationalism in the post-1918 period, Hobsbawm argues that the popular media of cinema, radio, and press had the ability to "make what were in effect national symbols part of the life of every individual, and thus to break down the divisions between the private and local spheres in which most citizens normally lived, and the public and national one" (Hobsbawm, 1990:142). Similarly, Jesus Martín-Barbero theorizes that the auditory and visual media of radio and cinema have the capacity to enter far-flung regions and localities and transform "the political idea of the nation into lived experience, into sentiment and into the quotidian" (Martín-Barbero, 1988:455-56).

In particular, the media of press, radio, and television represent a daily and even hourly intrusion into domestic space, thus breaking down the very distinction between public and private spheres. As Victoria De Grazia points out in the case of fascist Italy, these new means of communication—in particular, radio—were able to reach an entirely new audience —namely, women—on a daily basis. By entering the home and breaking down public-private divisions, Mussolini's government aimed "to national-ize Italian women, much as during the previous century . . . bourgeois gov-ernments sought to nationalize men" (De Grazia, 1992:6). Along the same lines, the new modalities of sight and sound used by cinema, radio, and television removed the barriers of literacy and schooling from individual participation in mass-mediated nationalism.

By arguing that communication media bring nationalism into the lives of common citizens, these scholars suggest that national identification is a constant part of quotidian experience. Although most nationalism schol-ars would agree that the degree of national identification and attachment ebbs and flows under different social conditions (for example, wartime or economic crisis), the work of Anderson, De Grazia, and others suggests that once the mass media are taken into account, it is impossible to deny the ubiquitous presence of nationalist discourse in the daily lives of most people. Hobsbawm, for example, suggests that it is not very important to know which private or state interests were controlling or exploiting the media for particular propaganda purposes, because "deliberate pro-paganda was almost certainly less significant than the ability of the mass media to make what were in effect national symbols part of the life of every individual" (Hobsbawm, 1990:142). In part, this is an accurate description of the media's ability to position national identity not as one kind of identi-fication among many, but as a ubiquitous and flexible mode of experience that organizes other forms of identification, including gender, sexuality, ethnicity, and religion.[2]

Not every kind of communication will create the conditions for national community. According to Anderson, the distinctively national orientation of the print medium is the product of capitalist exploitation of language-and culture-specific markets for mass communication, as well as the use of this communication technology by centralized state systems of administra-tion and control. Thus, the structure and control of media systems play a significant role in shaping both the style of communication and the kinds of community promoted through the media. As Breuilly argues in response to Deutsch's claim that increased social communication leads to national identification, "intensified communication between individuals and groups can as often lead to an increase in internal conflict as to an increase in soli-darity" (Breuilly, 1982). As noted in Chapter 1, all communication (even face-to-face communication) is subject to local interpretations. Although a particular representation of national community may be communicated through a centralized media system, this representation will have different meanings depending on the social contexts in which it is received. Thus, any community that depends on communication (as all communities do) will be subject to interference and mediations that disrupt and contradict dominant, idealized visions of that community.

The Radio Medium

Like the nation, the radio medium has both a hypermodern form and an antimodern orientation to the social changes and disruptions associated with it. This ambivalence is evident in various aspects of radio's technology and cultural form; for example, its nonreversible production of sound that moves endlessly through linear time. Radio's fleeting presence mimics the modern experience of reality as ephemeral and forward moving. This constant movement, or "flow," contributes to a sense of the immediacy, realism, and timeliness of radio content.[3] Flow also necessitates communicative techniques that can make meaning in such a mutable environment. Strategies such as interruption, repetition, simplicity, and standardization, for example, can be heard in a variety of radio techniques, including the use of sound montage and the placement of musical "bookends" at the beginning and end of radio programs (Benjamin, 1993; Altman, 1994). Along with technical and communicative constraints, flow is also conditioned by the political economy of broadcasting; in particular, the pressure to maximize profits from the commercial sale of audiences to advertisers (R. Williams, 1974; Edwards, 1997).

At the same time that flow is essential to radio's modern form, it also ties the medium to premodern practices of oral communication. As Jack Goody, Walter J. Ong, and others have argued, traditional oral cultures face a similar problem of making meaning out of the evanescent flow of sound and speech. Because purely oral language cannot store or transport information in the way that written language can, speakers are forced to find strategies to aid their recall and improve the transmission of ideas and narratives across time and space (Goody, 1977; Ong, 1995). The use of formulaic expressions, for example, provides a means of structuring and organizing ideas within the flow of oral speech. Thus, despite its use of written texts and other technological forms, radio performance is fundamentally dependent on oral formulas and standardized expressions to communicate effectively in a transitory sound medium. Although radio lacks the open and spontaneous performance contexts of primary orality, it can usefully be described as a medium of "secondary orality" (Ong, 1995).

A second salient feature of radio technology, along with its nonreversible flow, is its character as a purely aural medium. Lacking the visual modality, radio has traditionally drawn on cultural practices that could be translated into sound and speech, such as talk, storytelling, theater, literature, and music. As a highly flexible, portable, and easily reproducible art form, music is a particularly rich source of radio sound. From the beginning, broadcasters perceived music as the purest possible sound content for the medium and the "primary material" of Mexican radio (Gorostiza, 1932b; Arnheim, 1936). Second only to music, speech populates the radio medium with both the musical texture of the human voice and the deep historical, psychological, and social meanings activated by spoken language. By drawing on both oral traditions and literary texts, radio takes advantage of an "immense repository of expression" unavailable to purely visual media (Arnheim, 1936:25). Speech also does the important work of contextualizing radio sounds and giving them meaning—much in the same way that printed text accompanying photographs serves to specify and pin down the multiple meanings of the visual text (Barthes, 1977; Crisell, 1994).

Despite the lack of a shared performance context between the speaker and the audience, radio voices reproduce the immediate, tactile quality of primary orality in a number of ways. Roland Barthes's concept of the "grain" of the voice is particularly helpful in characterizing the felt "presence" of radio voices. Barthes describes the grain as "the body in the voice as it sings"; that is, the listener's sense of the physical presence of the performer in the sound of his or her voice (Barthes, 1990:299). He characterizes the grain as an "encounter" between the musical and emotive qualities of the voice and the semantics of language (Barthes, 1990:294). In this sense, radio voices produce both a felt texture and an intelligible meaning. Ong interprets the immediacy of radio voices somewhat differently, linking their felt presence to the enveloping qualities of sound in oral speech. According to Ong, radio talk has the same ability as oral speech to unite its audience "with themselves and with the speaker" by enveloping and immersing them in an experience larger than themselves (Ong, 1995:74).[4] Both Ong and Jürgen Habermas contrast the process of listening to the radio with the process of reading written or printed texts. Whereas reading "turns individuals in on themselves" and creates a context for abstract, critical reflection, radio listening forms hearers into sociable groups rather than reflective individuals (Habermas, 1989; Ong, 1995:136). Broadcasters actively work to re-create the sociability and interaction of oral settings by developing intimate, chatty forms of radio talk and using live audiences for radio performances (Scannell, 1991; Crisell, 1994; Lacey, 1994). In this way, radio's sound format gives listeners a sense of continuity with older forms of verbal intimacy and community.

The unique form of the radio medium shapes not only the style of performance but the mode of reception as well. First, the simultaneous access of vast numbers of listeners to a single radio content creates a virtual common space in which mass-mediated messages are experienced—and meanings interpreted—in parallel. In theory, these virtual meeting grounds could be as big or as small as the audience reached by an individual broadcasting station. In practice, however, these virtual commons tend to become co-terminous with the national territory. This is largely due to the dual forces of government regulation and commercial expansion working to codify and integrate a national market (see Chapter 3 for further discussion). As Rudolf Arnheim observes, despite the fact that "wireless eliminates not only the boundaries between countries but also between provinces and classes of society," it nonetheless enforces the "centralization, collectivism, and standardization" of national culture (Arnheim, 1936:238).

Second, radio's capacity to collapse space (and therefore time) and obliterate the distance between broadcasters and listeners adds to the palpable, even tactile, quality of radio communication. Although scholars sometimes describe radio sound as "disembodied" and "ethereal," many listeners report being bodily "moved" and "touched" by the intimate, emotional resonances of radio voices (Ramírez, 1933; Cantril and Allport, 1971). The experience of "feeling" the touch of a radio voice can be documented particularly well in listener letters responding to especially emotive music or effective radio speakers. For example, listeners responding to a program of popular music broadcast over government station XFX reported that they had been "transported" and "touched" by the familiar sounds of the music coming over their radios (OCR 1933h; see Chapter 4).

These aspects of the radio medium suggest two social implications: the creation of a new mode of mass-mediated intimacy and the formation of a new kind of collective space. The question of what kind of human contact was possible via radio broadcasting was a concern of the earliest North American communication scholars (Lippman, 1965; Cantril and Allport, 1971). Assessing the philosophies of these scholars and the culture of the radio era more broadly, John Durham Peters contends that this period was characterized by a sense of the "loss of the individual body" and a "longing for the supposed immediacy of the face to face" (Peters, 1996:108, 111). In other words, radio was experienced as a medium that denied, or superseded, physical intimacy and the corporeal embodiment of human speech and communication. Drawing on the theories of Ong and Barthes, however, I would argue that radio voices have a materiality that ties them directly to premodern, somatic modes of speech. Despite its incorporeity, radio sound directly provokes the corporeal experiences of hearing and feeling, as well as other kinds of bodily responses. For example, Peters cites Allison McCracken's work on sentimental singers, or "crooners," in early radio, who were viewed as scandalous because of the physical and emotional responses they provoked in swooning radio listeners. While Peters sees this as an example of the crooner's ability to compensate for radio's "communicative lacks" by foregrounding his own body and making himself more sincere and real to the listener, I view it as a telling example of radio's ability to blur humanity and technology. When crooners "made love" to the women in their radio audiences, it was not an ethereal communion but a shockingly corporeal one; and this sense of physical contact was a common feature of radio listening. Rather than feeling a "creepy unease about the new spectral bodies of broadcasting" (Peters, 1996:116), listeners grew accustomed to the touch of distant strangers. The scandal surrounding crooners was more likely a reaction to the particular subjects of this bodily touch; namely, young women. Crooners not only disrupted traditional, patriarchal control over women's bodies, but also promoted and celebrated the physical stimulation of young women.

At the same time that radio destabilized social relations, it articulated an antimodern vision of the communicative possibilities of the new medium. This antimodern perspective can also be seen in the way the mass-mediated, collective space created by radio voices disrupted Enlightenment categories. In particular, radio space created a new kind of collectivity that did not distinguish "public" from "private" in the traditional bourgeois sense (Habermas, 1989). In the new communicative space made available by radio broadcasting, no convincing distinction could be made between rational deliberation and emotional persuasion. In addition, public interests were inextricably intertwined with private concerns. While communication theorists from Marshal McLuhan to Jürgen Habermas have attempted to theorize this new mode of human collectivity, the historical perspective on the relationship between mass communication and nation attempted in the following chapters provides an alternative approach to understanding this new, mass-mediated form of community.

The Birth of Broadcasting

The development of Mexico's radio nation was contingent on a set of economic, technological, cultural, and political practices that came together as "broadcasting" in the years after World War I. In Mexico as in other countries, radio remained a means of point-to-point communication or wireless telegraphy from the time of the nation's first experimental radio transmissions in 1908 until the end of the First World War. Engineer Constantino de Tárnava and Dr. Gómez Fernández were among the first to experiment with voice broadcasting. The broadcasting practices that slowly matured over the course of the 1920s were shaped by three major historical developments originating in the nineteenth century: U.S. expansionism in Latin America, the rise of consumer product marketing and mass advertising, and the rise of an increasingly activist Mexican state. This chapter situates the specific history of Mexican broadcasting within these larger social processes in order to investigate the political trajectory and cultural orientation of the new medium.

U.S. Expansionism and the Rise of Broadcasting in the 1920s

Above all else, the birth of broadcasting in Mexico must be situated within the context of U.S. expansionism in Mexico and Latin America more generally. I use the term *expansionism* here rather than *imperialism* to distinguish my position from dependency and imperialism perspectives that view the expansion of U.S. and European interests abroad as a force that fully determined the limits and possibilities of Latin American development (Frank, 1969; Nordenstreng and Schiller, 1979). I agree with the basic framework of the imperialism perspective: advanced capitalist countries have achieved and maintained global positions of dominance by creating, controlling, and exploiting economic resources and markets in less-developed countries (Rosenberg, 1982; Brewer, 1990; Haynes, 1991). However, I disagree with the way that the effects of imperialism on exploited countries have been theorized. Indeed, scholars working within this framework have often neglected to examine the social dynamics of the dependent countries and therefore have failed to account for Latin American responses to conditions of imperialism (Fejes, 1981; Rivera-Perez, 1998).[1] Following Keith A. Haynes, I argue that historians must address the rise of social interests and alliances in Mexico that both accommodated themselves to and seriously challenged imperialist hegemony in the years following the Revolution (Haynes, 1991). For the purposes of this investigation, then, and in order to avoid confusion with deterministic models of imperialism, I employ the descriptively accurate (although undertheorized) term *expansionism* to characterize the government-sponsored extension of U.S. political and economic interests into Mexico.

U.S. expansionism in Mexico is not difficult to detect. By the end of the nineteenth century and the beginning of the twentieth, most Mexican industrial and economic development was shaped by direct or indirect U.S. economic investment. The U.S. investment in Latin America rose from $304 million in 1897 to $1.06 billion in 1908 and $1.64 billion in 1914. The 1914 figure represented about half of all U.S. foreign investment. Despite major economic disruptions, including the Mexican Revolution of 1910–16, U.S. economic penetration continued to increase during and after World War I as the position of European powers in the region weakened. By 1929 U.S. investment had increased to $2.08 billion (Fejes, 1986).

Investment in Mexico was part of a larger wave of U.S. investment in Latin America that benefited from strong government support during the late nineteenth and twentieth centuries. Under pressure from business associations at home, the government began to promote U.S. commercial interests abroad beginning in the 1890s. Key elements of this "promotional state" included a modern navy, new tariff strategies, the spread of the gold standard, and increased cooperation between government bureaucracy and business (Rosenberg, 1982; LaFeber, 1987). Part of what motivated this new strategy was the widely shared perception that the U.S. economy was in a stage of overproduction that required immediate expansion into new markets. In addition, by the early decades of the twentieth century, the British model of global expansion and dominion held enormous currency for U.S. officials and policy makers, who began to envision the United States as a force in world affairs.

In order to prove itself a worthy heir to Britain, the United States needed two things in addition to accumulated venture capital and a strong navy. First, it needed to carve out a sphere of influence. Due to proximity and the historical precedent of the Monroe Doctrine, this sphere came to focus on Latin America; however, the dream of an Asian sphere of influence was never entirely abandoned. Second, it needed to control a communication technology capable of aiding trade and coordinating production even in the far reaches of the "empire." While the British controlled telegraphic cables, the U.S. Navy found itself with a considerable head start in continuous-wave radio technology (the technology necessary for voice broadcasting) (Aitken, 1985).

The First World War gave new impetus to U.S. expansionism in Latin America because it virtually cut off European economic and political activities in the region. In the years immediately following the war, the U.S. government helped to create a private company, the Radio Corporation of America (RCA), to monopolize U.S. radio communication and force the British Marconi Corporation out of the United States. By 1921 RCA led European countries in the Latin American radio market.

The creation of RCA, and the development of broadcasting more generally, marked a new phase of close association and cooperation between the U.S. government and private interests. Focusing on the domestic sphere, Ellis Hawley uses the term *associative state* to describe a model of state building as one in which a "private government" of trade associations and professional groups supplemented the work of a small central government. This strategy was particularly evident at the Department of Commerce, where Secretary Herbert Hoover attempted to organize and coordinate self-regulation of the radio industry (Hawley, 1974). Focusing on the international arena, Emily Rosenberg uses the term *cooperative state* to characterize this new strategy. The cooperative state used governmental organizations and resources (especially the Commerce Department) to support North American businesses abroad. In particular, the cooperative state supplied corporations with market information and represented North American business interests in international trade negotiations and legal conferences (Rosenberg, 1982).

The role of the cooperative state in shaping international radio communication is evident in the series of Pan-American communication conferences beginning with the Inter-American Conference on Electrical Communications held in Mexico City in 1924. James Schwoch argues that the United States used the conference to launch a government-industry offensive aimed at shaping Latin American communication systems to serve North American commercial and strategic interests. During the proceedings, the U.S. delegates, including representatives from RCA, Westinghouse, AT&T, and All American Cables, called for radio frequencies to be allocated according to technological capabilities (giving the United States the lion's share of Western Hemisphere frequencies). They also opposed European models of state-controlled or publicly owned broadcasting systems and pressed for a system of private broadcasting licenses or concessions (Schwoch, 1990).

Schwoch reports that despite the efforts of the U.S. representatives, the Latin American delegates used the conference to voice their common interests. Among the resolutions supported by the Latin American delegates were the following declarations: that each government reserved for itself direct control of international electronic communication, that the media of electronic communication were public services, and that governments should promote free competition whenever feasible. In the end, the United States refused to ratify these resolutions, stating that they violated the American system of free competition. Ultimately only four Latin American countries ratified the convention resolutions; most decided to delay decisions about international communications until the 1927 conference in Washington, D.C.

In Schwoch's view, the 1924 conference was a failure—a failure that was actually a victory for the United States because the unratified resolutions adopted by the convention went against U.S. policy (Schwoch, 1990:74). After failing to control the outcome of the 1924 conference, North American delegates improved their lobbying efforts and their organization of the proceedings in order to dominate the 1927 negotiations. By the end of the decade, Schwoch concludes, "the American radio industry had suc-ceeded in shaping international radio policy in its own image" (Schwoch, 1990:78).

Along with setting the international stage for broadcasting, U.S. expan-sionism influenced the shape of Mexican economic development, in par-ticular, the development of the Mexican broadcasting industry. Foreign investment in Mexico, especially in infrastructural industries such as trans-portation, energy, and communication, was heavily promoted by the re-gime of Porfirio Díaz (1876–1911). As in the United States during this period, economic development under Díaz was characterized by the for-mation of oligopolies and monopolies. In Mexico, however, these giant, vertically integrated corporations were almost completely foreign owned. Stephen Haber notes that this process of industrialization by large for-eign corporations produced an extraordinarily lopsided form of economic development in Mexico. The advanced technologies used by foreign corpo-rations made the start-up costs of industry so high that "normal" competi-tion, investment, and development among domestic companies was impos-sible. Only a few giant Mexican firms succeeded, often as intermediaries or subsidiaries of foreign corporations. This lopsided process of development was further aggravated by the Díaz administration's policy of giving pref-erential treatment and special incentives to foreign businesses (Ruíz, 1980; Hart, 1987; Haber, 1989).

An exception to this model of development was Grupo Monterrey, a manufacturing group located in Monterrey, Nuevo León. For a variety of complex reasons, including proximity to North American capital and mar-kets, a dearth of mining and agricultural investment opportunities, and a unique entrepreneurial culture, Monterrey investors developed autono-mous, self-sustaining national industries while other parts of Mexico re-mained dominated by foreign-owned agricultural and mining ventures. The Monterrey Group successfully produced goods that had formerly been im-ported, such as glass and beer, and created a whole new national market for these products (Saragoza, 1990). By finding industrial niches that were not being effectively exploited by foreign corporations and by building on domestic capital resources, the Monterrey Group constituted an alternative model of economic development in Mexico.

In many ways, the broadcasting industry can be seen as straddling these two models of development. From the beginning, broadcasting was dominated by a small group of entrepreneurs who drew on foreign capital and aligned themselves with powerful financial and industrial families in Mexico. Mexico's early broadcasting entrepreneurs financed their stations with capital accumulated in related fields, such as newspaper publishing, electronics, and retail sales. The first commercial station, CYL, was launched in 1923 by Luis and Raul Azcárraga, retailers of North American radio parts and receivers, in partnership with the Mexico City newspaper *El Universal*. Another early station, CYB (later XEB), was started by a cigarette company, El Buen Tono, with French financial backing (Arredondo Ramírez and Sánchez Ruíz, 1986). The development of the broadcasting industry was directly linked to the Monterrey elite through Luis and Raul Azcárraga and, more important, their brother Emilio, who eventually became the most powerful figure in the radio industry.

Although he was not born in Monterrey, Emilio Azcárraga's career development closely followed the Monterrey model. Like other young members of the city elite, he was educated in the United States and became familiar with North American popular culture and commercial ventures (Saragoza, 1990). After starting out as the manager of a Monterrey Ford dealership, Azcárraga became a distributor for RCA-Victor and manager of a local radio station. With his marriage to the daughter of Patricio Milmo, the head of a large banking firm linked to French capital, Azcárraga gained access to significant financial resources (Baer, 1991). By 1930, Azcárraga had extended his success to the national level with the founding of station XEW—"La Voz de América Latina desde México" (The Voice of Latin America from Mexico)—in Mexico City.

Station XEW, like other early stations, was initiated with the specific aim of creating a demand for RCA radio receivers (Mejía Prieto, 1972; Fernández Christlieb, 1985; Fejes, 1986). Azcárraga continued to be affiliated with RCA (and later NBC and CBS) throughout the 1930s and 1940s, which helped to protect his position of dominance in the industry and limit the entry of competitors. At the same time, he built equally close ties with domestic capital (in part through strategic family marriages) and created a new national market for his unique product: commercial Mexican broadcasting.

During the 1920s, however, Mexican radio was still taking its first steps.

In 1923 the Ministry of Communications and Public Works authorized the first nonexperimental broadcasting stations, and by the end of the year four commercial stations and three government stations were on the air. Sixteen stations were broadcasting by 1926, and nineteen by 1929, the year Mexican stations received the "XE" and "XH" call letter designations. As these figures suggest, the broadcasting market remained limited during the 1920s: only an estimated twenty-five thousand radio sets were in operation in 1926, most located in Mexico City and other large urban areas.

Advertising and the Takeoff of Broadcasting

Hand in hand with U.S. expansionism, Mexican broadcasting was shaped by the development of U.S. mass-market advertising in the late nineteenth and early twentieth centuries. Like North American commercial expansion abroad, advertising was seen as a means of addressing the perceived crisis of overproduction in the United States. Advertising could not only increase product sales in a given market, it could actually create markets where none had existed before.

During World War I, the nascent North American advertising industry received inspiration for its international expansion from the U.S. Committee on Public Information (CPI), a propaganda agency designed to promote public support for the U.S. war effort at home and abroad. Described by its director as "the world's greatest adventure in advertising," the CPI's propaganda campaigns provided evidence of the power of verbal and visual persuasion on a mass scale and indicated that North American advertisers could be as successful abroad as they were at home. Both the state and the private sector could benefit by exporting "the American dream" for international consumption (Rosenberg, 1982). Although the history of U.S. advertising agencies in Latin America remains to be written, evidence suggests that they were becoming increasingly active in the region beginning in the 1920s. While the U.S. Commerce Department conducted feasibility studies of advertising in Latin America, advertising agencies for large-scale exporters such as Ford and General Motors established branch offices in a number of cities in the region (Fejes, 1986). Together with luxury consumer goods, which had always been sought by Latin American elites (by the 1920s these included automobiles and other consumer durables), the

1920s saw the marketing of cheap consumer goods in urban areas. Eye-catching advertisements for soaps, dental hygiene products, beauty aids, and processed foods and drinks became increasingly visible in newspapers and magazines, on billboards, and in shop displays.

The ear-catching capacities of radio were quickly exploited as well. Transnational corporations marketing cheap consumables, including Colgate Palmolive, Sydney Ross (Sterling Drug), and Coca-Cola, became the backbone of commercial radio broadcasting in Mexico. As the urban broadcasting market became more established in the early 1930s, commercial radio became an increasingly efficient means for advertisers to reach the urban masses. It is not surprising that these sponsors—most of whom had considerable radio experience in the United States—encouraged Mexican broadcasters to adopt and adapt radio formulas that had already proven successful in the North American market. For example, Colgate Palmolive pioneered the *radionovela* format (similar to the North American soap opera) and Coca-Cola promoted broadcasts of sports events on both Mexican and Cuban broadcasting stations (Salwen, 1994; Fox, 1997). Fueled by advertising revenues, radio broadcasting took off in the 1930s. Between 1930 and 1935 the number of radio stations climbed to more than 70 and the number of radio receivers grew to an estimated 250,000 sets. By the end of the decade, more than 120 radio stations were broadcasting in Mexico, and the number of radio sets was estimated at 450,000 (see Figure 3.1).

Although many prominent regional stations began operations during the early 1930s (including XET in Monterrey, XED in Guadalajara, and XEV in Vera Cruz), Mexico City became the undisputed power center of commercial broadcasting. At the epicenter of national broadcasting stood Azcárraga's station XEW, which became the most powerful radio station in the Western Hemisphere with two hundred kilowatts of power. By the late 1930s, Azcárraga and his company, the Mexican Music Company (an RCA subsidiary), had organized an XEW-led network encompassing fourteen regional stations. In 1938 he founded another flagship station in Mexico City, XEQ, and began to build a second national network. Mexican networks were very different from North American networks during the 1930s and 1940s, however. Because of the lack of infrastructure and the prohibitive cost of telephone lines, Azcárraga did not regularly use telephone connections to distribute programs to his affiliates.

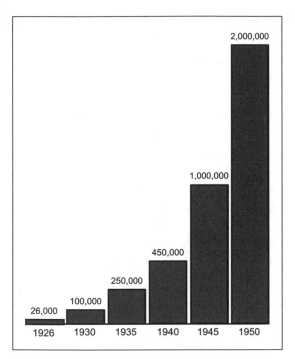

Figure 3.1 The estimated number of radio sets in Mexico, 1926–1950.

Instead, he simulated a broadcasting network by "bicycling" or shipping recorded programs between affiliate stations. Direct network connections were provided only occasionally for special programs (Cerwin, 1966; Mejía Barquera, 1989; Hayes, 1993a).

Although North American communication corporations such as RCA, GE, and Westinghouse were key to the development of Mexican broadcasting, they focused on providing broadcasting hardware and left the actual service of broadcasting in the hands of Mexican corporations and subsidiaries. Broadcasting companies such as NBC and CBS made no significant inroads into the Mexican broadcasting market before the early 1940s, although several radio historians report that XEW gained NBC affiliation as early as 1930 (Fernández Christlieb, 1985; Arredondo Ramírez and Sánchez Ruíz, 1986; Sinclair, 1986). Fernando Mejía Barquera suggests that the early "affiliation" between Azcárraga and NBC may simply have been a symbol of prestige for both organizations, and may have improved Azcárraga's access to RCA equipment and supplies. In any event, it is clear that it was not a North American–style network affiliation (Mejía Barquera, 1989; Hayes, 1993a).[2]

Barriers to North American network entry into Mexico were numerous during the 1930s. First, there were technological limitations that increased the costs of expansion into Mexico. Second, there were obvious limits to Mexico's market capacity compared with levels of consumption possible in the United States—even during the Depression years. Finally, there were perceived cultural barriers to entry that were, perhaps, magnified by the language barrier. Early radio theorists speculated that despite the medium's ability to make national borders obsolete, radio tended to be contained by the national market and oriented toward the "fictive ethnicities" deemed to be specific to each "national culture" (Balibar, 1991). In fact, this "fictive" barrier between Mexican and U.S. culture was being actively created during the 1930s by two actors with an interest in maintaining the uniqueness of the Mexican cultural sphere: Mexico's commercial radio broadcasters (principally the Azcárraga Group) and the Mexican state.

Although U.S. radio networks did not easily cross national boundaries, North American broadcasting models and formats were more mobile. Along with the influence of advertisers discussed above, Mexican broadcasters had ample opportunity to learn about North American commercial broadcasting formats and program types. Training sessions and tours of North American facilities were part of Azcárraga's ongoing relationship with RCA and NBC. In addition, the U.S. government directly and indirectly sponsored exchanges between Latin American and North American broadcasters. Such was the case during the 1927 Communications Conference in Washington, D.C., when Latin American broadcasters received elaborate facility tours and demonstrations from North American communication corporations and broadcasting networks (Schwoch, 1990). Later, during the propaganda offensive of World War II, the Office of the Coordinator of Inter-American Affairs encouraged and sponsored the training of Latin American broadcasters at facilities in the United States (CIAA, 1946b). In sum, the situation in Mexico was similar to the case of early European television described by Jérôme Bourdon: broadcasters' reliance on North American networks as a key professional resource was an important element in the early "Americanization" of their broadcasting programs and practices (Bourdon, 1998).

The State and the "Mexicanization" of Mexican Broadcasting

Despite the powerful commercial interests involved, the Mexican state also took a strong hand in radio development. Radio broadcasting came to maturity in Mexico at the same time that the post-revolutionary state achieved its modern institutional structure—during the early 1930s. As a consequence, the state showed considerable interest in radio as a powerful tool for modernizing the country, establishing political order, and building national cultural integration (Alisky, 1954; Mejía Barquera, 1989; Hayes, 1993a). In order to understand how radio development was shaped by this post-revolutionary context, it is helpful to look at the nineteenth-century roots of Mexican state building and the political and social transformations that accompanied the Revolution.

One of the legacies of the nineteenth-century Mexican state was an activist posture toward both capitalist development and national cultural integration. After the period of liberal reforms in the mid-nineteenth century (the Reforma) and the creation of the Liberal Constitution of 1857, Mexico had the political mechanisms in place to establish a decentralized, democratic republic. What it lacked was citizens. The vast majority of Mexicans were rural peasants without effective suffrage or access to national institutions. The landed and urban factions of the elite, on the other hand, struggled for power among themselves and expressed only modest commitment to the liberal-democratic experiment. Given the country's "ghost" democracy, then, it was relatively easy for Porfirio Díaz to seize power, neutralize the checks and balances of the Congress and Supreme Court, and centralize government power in the presidency (Meyer, 1977).

While the authoritarian Díaz regime promoted international investment and emphasized Mexico's need to "catch up with" the United States and Europe, it also engaged in nation building on a variety of fronts. Under Díaz, the central state promoted national integration and modernization through public works and infrastructural development, national education, and public art (Ruíz, 1992). According to Mary Kay Vaughan, the Díaz regime created a public school system that aimed to "modernize values and behavior within a capitalist framework and to train a hierarchically graded labor force appropriate to economic expansion" (Vaughan, 1982:75). As a whole, the political, cultural, and economic projects of the Díaz regime were designed to create and improve the conditions for private capital accumulation and capitalist enterprise in Mexico (Vaughan, 1982; Haber, 1989). The Mexican Revolution, initiated by Francisco I. Madero and his followers in 1910, attempted to dislodge the Díaz dictatorship and rebuild democratic institutions. Although questions of economic and social justice, as well as cultural identity, entered the revolutionary agenda with the mobilization of hundreds of thousands of peasants and workers in a protracted civil war, these interests were unable to control the final stages of the Revolution or the consolidation of state power. The revolutionary leaders who governed the Mexican polity after 1916 (Carranza, Obregón, and Calles) were strongly committed to modernization and capitalist development, and as a consequence, the post-revolutionary state retained a fundamentally liberal-bourgeois orientation (Ruíz, 1980; Leal, 1986). For example, the Constitution of 1917, despite using a radical rhetoric of peasant and worker rights, echoed the 1857 Constitution's support of capitalist development at the expense of these groups. The Revolution also failed to erase the enormous social gulf between the governing groups and the governed, creating a fertile environment for the development of an increasingly autonomous and authoritarian state in the post-revolutionary period (Meyer, 1977; Hamilton, 1982; O'Malley, 1986; Hart, 1987; Knight, 1987; Skidmore and Smith, 1997).

The post-revolutionary state, then, operated within a liberal-bourgeois framework when determining how to govern and regulate electrical communications such as radio broadcasting. The first recorded government ruling on radio was a 1916 decree by President Venustiano Carranza (1917–20) that required government authorization for commercial exploitation of radio and telegraphic resources (Mejía Barquera, 1989). This decree followed the liberal framework of the 1857 Constitution, which gave the central state the ability to grant private concessions for public transportation and communication enterprises. The Constitution of 1917 solidified this framework by giving the government monopoly control over radio and telegraphic services along with the power to grant private concessions for the commercial development of these media. In this way, radio (along with other industries of communication and transportation) was treated as an essential infrastructural industry in which the central government took a direct strategic interest. It was also subject to government regulation in order to ensure the even and efficient flow of commerce. Following a "common carrier" regulatory logic, electrical communications were required to be "open to all equally, without any kind of distinction" in the general interests of national commerce (Horwitz, 1989; Mejía Barquera, 1989). In 1922 President Álvaro Obregón (1920-24) exhorted Mexican citizens to establish radio stations, indicating the state's interest in the development of the new medium, and in 1923 Mexico City broadcasters formed the Radio League to lobby the government for radio regulations that would promote commercial broadcasting (Mejía Barquera, 1989). The regulatory framework that emerged in Mexico was also greatly influenced by international negotiations over radio communication; namely, the 1924 Conference on Electrical Communications discussed earlier. Approaching the conference from a Mexican perspective, Fernando Mejía Barquera shows that it had important implications for Mexican broadcasting not considered in Schwoch's analysis of the convention. Mejía Barquera points out that whereas the 1924 conference resolutions might be considered a failure from an international perspective, in Mexico they became the basis for the country's 1926 Law of Electric Communications. Both the conference resolutions and the 1926 communication law awarded the Mexican government a significant measure of control over the radio medium, although this was limited by the reality of U.S. expansionism in Mexico. In other words, while the Mexican state could not afford to exclude North American capital and technology from the development of Mexican broadcasting, it opposed the absolute control of radio communications by U.S. corporations and demanded regulatory supervision over the national broadcasting system (Mejía Barquera, 1989).

The 1926 Law of Electric Communications declared the radio spectrum to be a national resource, created a system of concessions for commercial broadcasters, mandated that only Mexican citizens could own or operate radio stations, and authorized the Ministry of Communications and Public Works to implement and oversee these regulations. In addition, the law gave the federal government total control over the radio system in times of public emergencies and prohibited all transmissions that threatened state security or public order or "attacked the established government in any way" (Alisky, 1954; Arredondo Ramírez and Sánchez Ruíz, 1986; Mejía Barquera, 1989:43).

The state's general interest in promoting the national integration of broadcasting was coupled with a growing need, under conditions of mass political participation, to build national consensus for state policies and actions. The state used radio regulations to establish its own broadcasting stations and to access privately licensed stations during times of national crisis. In addition, the central government built both formal and informal relations with commercial networks and broadcasting organizations. Once the state gained a privileged position of access to the radio broadcasting medium, it used a discourse of revolutionary nationalism to present its highly political and interested voice as a *neutral* one that stood for "national" interests and goals that were "above politics" (O'Malley, 1986).

Although the 1920s was a decade of crisis and instability for the Mexican government, there is no reason to assume that the radio law of 1926—or the commercial trajectory of Mexican broadcasting in general—was counter to the interests of the Mexican state. Some scholars have argued that the economic and political crises of the period, combined with Mexico's need for the United States to recognize the revolutionary government, forced the state (against its better interests) to establish a commercial radio system and open the medium to North American corporations (Fernández Christlieb, 1985; Arredondo Ramírez and Sánchez Ruíz, 1986; Baer, 1991). But there is evidence to the contrary suggesting that the state actively promoted commercial broadcasting as early as 1916. Given the Mexican government's commitment to capitalist development, it is not surprising that it encouraged the participation of North American media corporations in Mexican radio and looked positively on the model of advertising-supported broadcasting that they promoted (Mejía Barquera, 1989). Indeed, as Nora Hamilton and others argue, the Mexican state was itself a creation of foreign capital and dependent capitalist relations and therefore lacked complete autonomy from such "foreign" interests (Hamilton, 1982). Although the Mexican state attempted to regulate North American participation and foster a national broadcasting market, its developmental goals required foreign capital and technology.

The broadcasting policies and activities of the political regime of Plutarcho Elias Calles (1924–34)[3] continued to promote the expansion and consolidation of commercial broadcasting ventures at the same time that they built a larger and more influential position for the central government in broadcasting. The 1931 and 1932 radio laws replaced the system of one-year broadcasting permits with concessions lasting up to fifty years, declared that radio studios could not be located on foreign soil, and required all stations to broadcast in Spanish. Non-Spanish-language broadcasts required special government permission.[4] These regulations also required concessionaires to transmit all government messages free of charge, including ten minutes of Health Department bulletins each day (Norris, 1962). The 1931 communication law included a preamble explicitly stating that regulations such as the one prohibiting radio studios on foreign soil were made on "nationalistic grounds" in order to defend "the national culture" (Barbour, 1940:101).

By the early 1930s, the 1926 ruling prohibiting citizens from using the broadcasting medium to attack the established government "in any way" had been expanded and clarified to prohibit Mexicans from engaging in political discourse (*hacer política*) over the airwaves. With this ruling, the use of the airwaves for political discourse became "an exclusive right of the state" (Mejía Barquera, 1989:51). The political climate of Mexican radio at that time is perhaps best illustrated by the Communist Party broadcast transmitted over station XEW on November 7, 1931, which took place under unique conditions: three party members tied up an XEW technician and took over the transmitter by force. The event was reported in the mainstream press as well as the Communist Party paper, *El Machete*. Under the headline "The Voice of the Communist Party of Mexico from 'X.E.W.,' " *El Machete* described the broadcast as a ten-minute speech delivered just after 9:00 P.M. during a well-advertised concert. Given on the anniversary of the Russian Revolution, the speech attacked Yankee imperialism, defended the USSR, and blamed the repressive Calles dictatorship for the misery of Mexico's masses. The perpetrators of this "audacious strike" (*golpe de audacia*) escaped before the police arrived and were not apprehended (*El Machete*, 1931). Needless to say, XEW and other stations increased their security after that. Only under extraordinary circumstances, then, could alternative political voices be heard over the radio medium.

Along with its enhanced regulatory role, the state also embarked on an intensified project of political and cultural propaganda broadcasts during the 1930s. In 1931 the Partido Nacional Revolucionario (PNR), the government's official party, initiated station XE-PNR (later XEFO). Although not a state-owned station, it was operated by the PNR and conveyed official doctrine. According to Manuel Jasso, the PNR's secretary of propaganda and culture, the goal of XEFO was to strengthen the party organization and increase national solidarity by establishing a channel of daily contact with the Mexican people. The specific aim of XEFO broadcasts was to achieve what Jasso described as "the spiritual incorporation of the proletarian masses by means of art, literature and music" (Mejía Barquera, 1989:55–56).

In Mejía Barquera's view, XEFO's nationalistic content had one objective: to co-opt the political and social aspirations of the Mexican people to serve the political ends of the PNR. To make sure its message got across, the PNR distributed radios and loudspeakers to agricultural communities and working-class neighborhoods. As the PNR statement indicates, however, these political ends were tied to an essentially cultural project: the creation and dissemination of a body of art, literature, and music capable of integrating all Mexicans into a state-guided national culture.

The activities of station XFX, which was operated by the Ministry of Public Education (SEP), also increased considerably during the early 1930s. In 1933, XFX expanded to a full broadcast day that included daytime courses in language, history, and hygiene for schoolchildren together with evening programs of music and literature. The station aired information about a wide variety of government services, policies, and mandates, and gave the state a new and dynamic means of reaching its citizens. Despite the relatively low audience garnered by this five-hundred-watt station (compared with the powerful commercial broadcasters), XFX established an important example of government programming and nationalistic propaganda that influenced both future government stations and commercial broadcasters (see Chapter 4). Station XFX also played a significant part in the government's intensified campaign of socialist education and acculturation beginning in 1934 and 1935. For example, the station provided a forum for a number of radio conferences on Marxism, Leninism, and competing social theories—under the auspices of the SEP (Arredondo Ramírez and Sánchez Ruíz, 1986; Mejía Barquera, 1989; Loyo, 1990).

The Mexican broadcasting system took on a distinctly nationalistic orientation within the liberal-bourgeois framework that guided its development between 1920 and 1934. Approaching radio broadcasting as a strategic resource and medium of national commerce, the Mexican government used its regulatory powers to limit broadcasting to national subjects and promote the growth and development of a nationwide broadcasting system. Faced with the efforts of U.S. media corporations to expand into Mexican broadcasting (with considerable help from the U.S. government), the Mexican state took steps to guide and limit the direct role of those corporations in order to promote a nationally integrated radio system. The state also became a broadcaster in its own right in order to build political and cultural consensus. Ultimately, the state gained a position of privileged access to the national broadcasting system and played a significant role in shaping the development of commercial broadcasting within the larger context of U.S. expansionism and mass-market advertising.

Broadcasting the Revolution

At the beginning of the 1930s, the Mexican state energetically turned to radio broadcasting as a tool for creating and disseminating a national culture. Station XFX, operated by the Ministry of Public Education, was one of the earliest government broadcasting projects to develop a cultural policy aimed at unifying the country's culturally diverse and geographically dispersed citizens. Through a program of music designed to celebrate a national musical heritage, XFX created a model of nationalist discourse that influenced both government and commercial broadcasting in Mexico throughout the twentieth century. This chapter traces the institutional development of government broadcasting, analyzes XFX cultural policies and musical programs, and explores audience reactions to XFX broadcasts.

Government Broadcasting for National Integration: The Case of Station XFX

Station XFX, founded in 1924 by María Luisa Ross under the original call letters CZE, emerged during a tumultuous period of expansion and change at the Ministry of Public Education. The station's broadcasts remained irregular until Narciso Bassols, the first Marxist to hold high government office in Mexico, took over the directorship of the SEP in the early 1930s. Bassols's tenure at the SEP (1931–34) was marked by strident efforts to secularize primary and secondary schooling, expand rural education, and improve the social and economic conditions of Mexico's popular classes (Ortiz H., 1960; Britton, 1971). His anticlericalism and social activism were accompanied by a strong nationalist discourse and a concern for the "construction of nationality" through education (Luna Arroyo, 1934). Although Bassols promoted a form of rural education that emphasized the economic and social empowerment of peasants and laborers, he continued to view the nation-building process through a "civilizing" framework: "Our education must realize a synthesis of the two cultures, conserving the positive values of the indigenous races and taking from western civilization, with its technical resources and the possibilities that technology presents, all that which will strengthen our Indians converting them into a race physically vigorous and mechanically capable of producing riches in great abundance" (Britton, 1971:47). As this statement suggests, Bassols's radical politics was accompanied by a conservative, bourgeois cultural perspective on Mexico's indigenous people. According to Barry Carr, this perspective was not uncommon among Mexican Marxists and leftist leaders of the 1930s, many of whom expressed the need to "uplift" and "civilize" the Mexican masses (Carr, 1994).

In an effort to build a national, unified system of rural education, Bassols encouraged the use of radio broadcasting and "brought educational radio from a marginal activity to a position of importance in the Ministry's rural programs" (Britton, 1971:51–52). Under the direction of young Agustín Yáñez and the Office of Cultural Radiotelephony (OCR), the SEP developed a regular broadcasting service as a means of standardizing rural education and integrating rural communities into national life.[1] Although the policy vision of XFX officials was a national one, the actual reach of station policies was constrained by the limited resources of government broadcasters. Like most government agencies, the Office of Cultural Radiotelephony operated on a shoestring budget; it could afford only a low-power radio transmitter (five hundred watts) and limited programming resources. The low level of radio interference during these early years, however, permitted the station's weak Mexico City transmitter to reach most of the country's Central Valley (where almost 40 percent of the nation's population lived) by day and to blanket much of the republic by night (Kuhlmann, Alonso, and Mateos, 1989).

Because no surveys or estimates of the XFX audience survive in the SEP archive, it is impossible to measure its size or composition accurately. However, by looking at the general characteristics of radio listening during this period it is possible to speculate about which Mexicans were most likely to have listened to station XFX. There were probably about 250,000 radio receivers in Mexico in 1935 (the majority located in urban areas), so most of the XFX radio listeners would have been Mexico City residents. Although most radios in private homes would have been owned by professionals or other upper-class residents, it is likely that many urban dwellers listened in public places such as bars, restaurants, community centers, and schools (Schwoch, 1990). Even though XFX would have drawn only a fraction of the audience that the high-powered commercial stations were able to reach, it probably received the particular attention of educators, government bureaucrats, and other prominent citizens. In addition, XFX was able to increase both its transmission power and its audience size by broadcasting programs of particular importance through network hookups with PNR station XEFO and other stations.

The impoverished condition of most of the Mexican countryside limited radio listening in rural areas. Government programs that distributed radios to rural schools and communities made it possible for XFX to reach some rural listeners in Mexico's central and southern regions, however. In 1933, for example, the SEP donated seventy-five radios to rural schools in the central region, with each radio set to the frequency of station XFX. Overall, hundreds of radios were distributed to agricultural communities and urban working-class neighborhoods by the SEP, PNR, and other government agencies (Mejía Barquera, 1989). Thus, although XFX did not reach a comprehensive national audience, it had a significant presence in Mexico City and the central region as one of only a few dozen stations operating in Mexico during radio's early years.

The broadcasting mission of station XFX was to provide a channel for public information from all government agencies and to produce its own educational and cultural programs. It also served as a testing ground for later government broadcasting projects. When the station initiated a full broadcast day in 1933, educational programs aimed primarily at school children were aired during the day, and cultural programs aimed at the general public were broadcast during the evening hours. The XFX daytime schedule included courses in language, history, geography, and hygiene, as well as more broadly "cultural" programs such as a news program and a

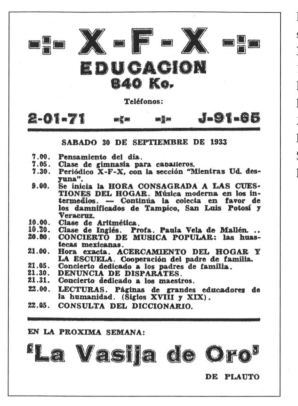

Figure 4.1 A program schedule for SEP station XFX, September 30, 1933. (Oficina Cultural Radiotelefónica, Programas, expediente 33, caja 1315. Archivo Histórico de la Secretaría de Educación Pública, Mexico City.)

Home Hour program aimed at Mexico City housewives. The evening schedule was devoted predominantly to musical programs but also included conferences, literature readings, and radio theater (see Figure 4.1). Among the many prominent educators and intellectuals who planned and participated in XFX's cultural programs were Germán List Arzurbide, Maricio Magdaleno, and Rodolfo Usigli; numerous musicians and composers, including Carlos Chávez and Silvestre Revueltas, took part as well. In 1936 Usigli became director of the Department of Press and Publicity (which operated station XEDP), and Magdaleno went on to coordinate broadcasts of the *National Hour* (*La hora Nacional*) between 1943 and 1950 (*Encyclopedia de México*, 1987).

The broadcasting policy of XFX can be traced through a series of reports and memos that were generated by the staff of the Office of Cultural Radiotelephony when they met in the spring of 1932 to reorganize the radio education project. Through a programming schedule designed both to educate and to entertain, station officials hoped to bring about a "moral, economic and material coming together [*acercamiento*] of the people of the country" (Yáñez, 1932:1). The OCR aimed to extend the government's cultural influence into agrarian communities and worker organizations by disseminating a "wholesome" national culture to the farthest corners of the republic (Bellas Artes, 1932a, 1932d; Gorostiza, 1932a). A station announcement proclaimed that the objective of XFX cultural programs was to build "direct relations between the whole of the Mexican family and the educational leaders in whom the government of the republic has placed the standard of national culture" (OCR, 1933i). In this way, the station's broadcasting policy aimed to achieve two goals that Radio Office bureaucrats viewed as fundamentally linked, if not actually equivalent: building national cultural unity and extending the social influence of the SEP (and the state more generally) in the everyday lives of Mexican citizens. One party official noted that the dissemination of art, music, and literature through PNR station broadcasts offered an important means of "incorporating" the Mexican masses into the official political culture. Using the instrumental language of state power, the declaration establishing the Autonomous Department of Press and Publicity (DAPP; see Chapter 5) maintained that without such cultural propaganda "it is not possible to infiltrate the public spirit with the stimulus that is necessary to bring it to cooperate" (Cárdenas, 1936; Mejía Barquera, 1989).

The Cultural Policy of Station XFX: Defining Musical Nationalism

The station's nationalist policy was most clearly elaborated in the case of musical programming, which OCR officials described as a "necessity of human life and primary material of radio" (OCR, 1933f). Music filled the bulk of the station's prime broadcasting hours. The decision to focus on music rather than dramatic forms was a significant one. In part, it was influenced by the prevalence of music in Mexican life and the richness of the country's musical traditions. Music was also a logical choice because it was much less expensive to produce than drama, especially when it was available on records.[2] As Mary Kay Vaughan points out, however, the decision was also shaped by the SEP's interest in music as a means of social control. In the view of some SEP administrators, music had the power to pacify social tensions and incorporate the lower classes into the social hierarchy by connecting them to a state-sanctioned model of national community (Vaughan, 1982). One Radio Office strategist described the objective of the station's musical broadcasts as "the conquest of the audience" (*la conquista de auditorio*) (Gorostiza, 1932b:11). The OCR's notion of cultural "conquest" was a dual one that aimed to incorporate the country's "uncivilized" rural and urban masses as well as to rescue and recuperate the corrupted, commercial culture of urban elites.

Significant (though unacknowledged) contradictions developed in the discourse of SEP nationalists, however, as they tried to determine which elements of Mexican music would best typify or represent the nation. XFX broadcasters consistently identified popular music (*música popular*) as an authentic product of Mexico's popular classes—both urban and rural—and celebrated Mexico's peasant and worker communities as "the places where our music was born" (Rodríguez Lomeli, 1933b:5). Although bourgeois nationalists saw working-class and peasant culture as being far removed from the "noble" and idealized indigenous past, they celebrated popular culture as one of the last places where indigenous sentiments, tones, expressions, and gestures could still be found (Vaughan, 1982; Moreno Rivas, 1989). On taking a closer look at Mexico's rural communities, however, OCR nationalists could not easily navigate the tensions between praising and debasing popular culture that they felt as bourgeois intellectuals. While praising campesino culture as the source of Mexico's "greatest popular art," they simultaneously described rural peasants as being devoid of musical talents and traditions. For example, as OCR bureaucrats debated the type of musical programming that would be most appropriate for the station, one official said: "As for the quality of the music, I believe it is necessary to offer uniformly the best ancient and modern music, without making concessions of any kind. . . . Somebody will object that it is a monstrosity to make a peasant listen to Stravinsky or Honnegger, but not only is it not a monstrosity, but I would say that, having listened to nothing, the campesino is more prepared than anyone to listen to this class of music" (Gorostiza, 1932b). Seamlessly, the rural peasants who were hailed as the authors of Mexico's authentic music were also described as having "listened to nothing." In a similar vein, a rural teacher wrote that XFX broadcasts would provide a means of awakening artistic talents in Mexico's Indians, whom he described as "so separated from musical elements" (OCR, 1933f). In the contradictory language of SEP officials and teachers, Mexico's rural communities were paradoxically both rich in musical traditions and barren of musical talent.

The Tension between "Authenticity" and "Civilization" in Mexican Nationalism

The unresolved—and seemingly unproblematic—contradictions expressed by OCR bureaucrats reflect an underlying tension in their nationalist vision between the search for an authentic national identity and the imperative to articulate culture in terms of civilization. This tension can be traced back to the complex and contradictory discourse of Creole nationalism articulated by Mexico's ruling groups in the late eighteenth and early nineteenth centuries. The contradictions at the heart of Creole nationalism persisted even after independence: Mexico's leaders needed to identify with the indigenous past in order to legitimate their autonomy and distinct national identity; but at the same time they were culturally, institutionally, and economically committed to a European worldview (OCR, 1933f; Brading, 1985; Ruíz, 1992). In the 1920s and 1930s, Mexico's bureaucrats and intellectuals continued to face formidable contradictions in their own nationalist ideology between the intense search for an authentic Mexican identity unleashed by the Revolution and the bourgeois preference for European culture.

It is possible to clarify this contradiction by comparing Mexican bourgeois nationalism with the early history of African American nationalism. The latter highlights the tension between the need for an authentic ethnic or racial identity (on which to base the autonomy of the national community) and the desire to position the nation on a "progressive" and "civilized" cultural trajectory. In his study of black nationalism between 1850 and 1925, Wilson Jeremiah Moses argues that bourgeois nationalists, most notably W. E. B. DuBois, were torn between a celebration of racial unity or "mystical racial chauvinism" and a concern with "uplifting" and acculturating the black race to the standards of European civilization. For nationalists like DuBois, elements of African American popular culture that reflected an African heritage could become viable building blocks for black nationalism only after they had been "improved" to reflect bourgeois moral and aesthetic standards (Moses, 1988). Kathy Ogren argues that it was not until the post–World War I period of the Harlem Renaissance that a new generation of black intellectuals such as Zora Neal Hurston and Langston Hughes began to celebrate African American popular culture, including jazz music, as a direct source of black cultural identity— one that stood in defiant contrast to long-standing notions of bourgeois "civility" (Ogren, 1989). The nationalism of Mexico's bourgeois intellectuals followed a similar logic. One of the most influential formulations of a "mystical racial chauvinism" in Mexico was José Vasconcelos's concept of the "cosmic race." Vasconcelos, who directed the SEP in the early 1920s, expressed his vision of the Mexican race as a transcendent Hispanic cultural tradition (*hispanidad*) that emphasized Mexico's Spanish and Latin-European cultural identity. This Hispanic-mestizo racial vision argued that Mexico's Spanish, rather than Indian, cultural heritage would provide the only viable basis for a meaningful national culture (Partin, 1973; Vázquez Valle, 1989). While some Mexican intellectuals of the 1920s and 1930s, including Manuel Gamio and Carlos Chávez, shifted the focus of Mexican ethnicity away from hispanidad and toward *indigenismo* (a celebration of indigenous, pre-Colombian culture), most of them continued to interpret indigenous culture in much the same way that DuBois interpreted African American culture: according to bourgeois traditions of beauty and art (Porritt, 1983; Moreno Rivas, 1989). For example, Anthony Smith observes that anthropologist Manuel Gamio "recognized the beauty and the worth of Indian folk arts and crafts" while he simultaneously "condemned them as expressions of backwardness" (Smith, 1990). Even as Gamio celebrated the Indian culture that was rejected by Vasconcelos, he was unable to reconcile his interest in the authentic ethnic roots of Mexican culture with his belief that a legitimate culture should meet the standards of Western civilization.

This complex history of class and race relations is essential for understanding the antimodern tensions at the heart of XFX musical nationalism. While compelled by the populist impulse of revolutionary nationalism to celebrate the "authentic popular," Mexican bureaucrats were likewise shocked by the inability of these popular practices to meet the standards of bourgeois culture. As Vaughan observes, the SEP's project of cultural nationalism was guided by "an intellectual elite still beholden to metropolitan [European] standards of art and repulsed by much of the real popular culture of Mexico" (Vaughan, 1982:239). Mexican nationalists undertook a complex process of selection and transformation in order to adapt aspects of the popular to their larger project of cultural nationalism.

XFX Musical Nationalism as a "Selective Tradition"

Although bureaucrats at the Office of Cultural Radiotelephony widened the lens of national culture to include some elements of Indian culture along with the Hispanic tradition, they remained committed to the idea of elevating and uplifting the ethnic culture in order to achieve a European-style Mexican civilization. In the reports of OCR administrators, the objective of national education was always tied to a project of cultural improvement. One official noted that by presenting an uplifted version of Mexican culture, station XFX would help to replace the false and "deformed" stereotypes of Mexicans so prevalent in Europe and the United States. By "obtaining the elevation of the aesthetic culture of each locale and elevating their regional arts" (Bellas Artes, 1932c), station XFX broadcasts would "improve" popular culture and create "a real, favorable concept of the culture of the Mexican people" (Bellas Artes, 1932b). Through radio programs that transformed Mexico's popular regional cultures, OCR nationalists aimed to build an authentic, yet civilized and respectable, national culture.

The cultural practices that shaped musical programming at XFX can be described by Raymond Williams's term *selective traditions*: traditions that select and reinterpret popular cultural practices in terms of the cultural system of the dominant social groups (Williams, 1977). XFX programs frequently reorganized, "cleaned up," and "uplifted" the musical practices of common people in order to standardize and institutionalize them for new national purposes (Hobsbawm and Ranger, 1983; Vázquez Valle, 1989). A closer look at XFX program objectives reveals the antimodern orientation of this process of selection and interpretation.

In planning a program schedule that would include popular music, OCR officials first had to distinguish between the potential beauty of popular music and what they perceived as the "tainted" social contexts in which it was created—specifically the cantinas and *pulquerías*, which were viewed as "traditional centers of debasing escapism" as well as troubling zones of sexual and moral turpitude (Booth, 1941). The SEP took steps to assert itself as a mediator between popular culture and the people in order to remove these cultural forms from the "dirty" social contexts in which they flourished. One rural teacher suggested that the SEP should create its own institutions of popular music in order to "keep the older people away from the cantinas and keep the young people from getting into the habit of frequenting them" (Badillo, 1933). By purifying popular music and removing it from the corrupt settings of peasant and working-class conviviality, OCR officials believed they could transform it into a viable medium for national integration (OCR, 1933c, 1933d).

Station XFX nationalists also viewed commercialization as a source of pollution of Mexico's popular music because it subjected Mexican music to foreign musical styles and the "corrupted whim of the public" (OCR, 1933f). The perspective of OCR administrators paralleled the view of a prominent music critic who argued that the "kitsch" of commercial radio was infecting the performers of Mexico's authentic popular music like a deadly virus. "This is true particularly of players of Huapangos," he observed, "whose collective rhythmical devices are so delicate that Blas Galindo, the young Indian composer, assures me a week of radio work is sufficient to ruin a group forever" (Bowles, 1940–41:225). In the view of OCR bureaucrats, XFX was the lone bastion against this spreading disease. "With the well-defined aim of offsetting the effects of American jazz," one official said, "... we are developing an especially nationalistic program, broadcasting every Thursday Mexican music and closing the concert with the National Anthem" (Bellas Artes, 1932b:9). For XFX bureaucrats, the term *jazz* became a code word for all the "vile" foreign rhythms, so popular in urban areas, that seemed to be threatening the authenticity and beauty of Mexico's own music.

In sum, the construction of a national musical tradition required a transformation of popular musical forms into hegemonic cultural practices that could be used to support and legitimate the state. The musical programming of station XFX represents what Stuart Hall has described as an effort to "disorganize and reorganize popular culture; to enclose and confine its

definitions and forms within a more inclusive range of dominant forms"
(Hall, 1981:233). In her study of elite representations of popular culture
in Mexico during this period, Irene Vázquez Valle concurs that members
of the elite deformed popular expressions, extracted them from their social contexts, elevated them as symbols of the post-revolutionary state, or
reduced them to mere curiosities (Vázquez Valle, 1989). Although SEP nationalists cast themselves in the role of protectors of Mexican culture, they
transformed popular musical practices just as much as their commercial
counterparts by making them conform to European musical conventions.
SEP officials were threatened by commercialization not just because it introduced corrupting foreign influences, but because it also exposed Mexican traditions to the tyrannical "whim" of the masses of uneducated, lower-
class Mexicans whose ethnic backgrounds were largely non-European
(OCR, 1933f).

On the other hand, the activities of Mexican nationalists must also be
recognized as genuine efforts to celebrate and preserve popular cultural expressions. SEP bureaucrats and other state nationalists did, in fact, save
some aspects of Mexican popular culture from being obliterated by the
"commercial cultural deluge" from the United States (O'Malley, 1986:
121). In addition, and perhaps more important, the musical programs of
station XFX legitimated and celebrated popular cultural forms that had
been marginalized within Mexican culture for decades and actively scorned
by the Mexican upper classes. As Vázquez Valle points out, it was through
the efforts of intellectuals like those at the SEP that "popular culture finally
entered the stage of Mexican culture" (Vázquez Valle, 1989:7). However,
the recognition that this was a moment of cultural inclusion should not
blind us to the processes of transformation that made this inclusion palat-
able and even possible.

XFX Musical Programs: Creating a New Mestizo Nationalism

A closer look at XFX musical programming reveals how the selective tradition of mestizo music worked to bridge the gap between authenticity
and civilization in state nationalism. Overall, the format of OCR musical
programs reveals two general objectives. First, OCR officials drew on the
country's regional musical genres—from *huapangos* to *jarabes* to *danzas*—

to create a "panorama" of regional musical traditions. This musical panorama positioned regional songs as inspiring examples of a larger body of
Mexican national music. Second, XFX concerts aimed to connect these
exemplary strands of Mexican music to an evolving body of European classical and modern art music.

The station's mestizo nationalism was expressed in a variety of musical forms ranging from symphonic to orchestral to small group (*conjunto*)
music. An analysis of OCR program schedules shows that evening musical programs fell into five general categories. By far the largest single category was European and Mexican art music, which constituted 62 percent of all evening musical programs. "Art music" refers to symphonic and
chamber music composed in a predominantly European harmonic and
rhythmic style. The second largest category, which made up 18 percent
of evening musical programs, was music characterized as "Mexican" or
"popular." Music performed by bands (which included military-style
marches and some popular tunes) made up 7 percent of all evening musical programs. A broad category of "international popular music" made up
5 percent, and another 8 percent of evening musical programs could not
be categorized for lack of information (OCR, 1933b).[3]

Despite the different types of music broadcast, the majority of XFX
musical programs shared a single ideological project: the celebration of an
idyllic premodern world through the presentation of a selective tradition
of regional popular music. Yolanda Moreno Rivas argues that Mexico's
art music composers incorporated the popular music of rural mestizos
and Indians in an effort to "recuperate for art a vanishing space: the pre-
capitalist rural world" (Moreno Rivas, 1989:171). Within this recuperated
space Mexican composers envisioned a harmonious social world characterized by the "joy, simplicity, nobility, and energy" of Mexican popular culture (*lo popular mexicano*) (Moreno Rivas, 1989). Manuel Peña uses similar terms to describe Mexico's commercial ranchera music, which painted
an idealized picture of rural life on the hacienda and celebrated the values
of "manliness, self-sufficiency, candor, simplicity, [and] sincerity" (Peña,
1985:10–11).

This focus on a beautiful and innocent rural landscape was in fact the
product of a modern, capitalist nostalgia (Clark, 1969; R. Williams, 1973).
As Williams describes it, this idealization of the rural world reflected "an

ideological separation between the processes of rural exploitation, which have been, in effect, dissolved into a landscape, and the register of that exploitation in the law courts, the money markets, the political power, and the conspicuous expenditure of the city" (R. Williams, 1973:46). This collapsed rural landscape became a site for the projection of a "former innocence": a place to represent a harmonious and transcendent vision of the national community. For modern bourgeois nationalists, the cultural themes and practices of the rural world seemed to stand "outside the present flow of history"—at a distance from contemporary political conflicts (Mosse, 1991:6). Representations of rural culture, with their unique ability to transcend conflict and promote national unity, played a central role in the musical discourse of state broadcasters.

European and Mexican Art Music

The classical and modern art music that dominated the evening hours included daily piano concerts, performances by the XFX Radio Orchestra, and concert series by the National Classical Quartet, the Popular Evening School of Music, the National Conservatory, and the Mexican Symphony Orchestra. Under the direction of Carlos Chávez, the Mexican Symphony began broadcasting over station XFX and XEFO during the early 1930s as part of an effort to popularize symphonic music among Mexico's dispersed rural population (Chávez, 1945).

While XFX concerts were filled with European music—including heavy doses of Beethoven, Chopin, Debussy, and Stravinsky—the overall focus of the station's art music was on the creation of a modern, pan-Hispanic musical culture. For example, Spanish art music inspired by folk and popular tunes (such as Ravel's *Bolero*) was repeatedly featured in XFX concerts together with compositions by Mexico's own composers, most notably Silvestre Revueltas, Carlos Chávez, and Manuel Ponce. Weekly concert series combined, for example, the music of Beethoven, Chopin, and Debussy with the works of Spanish composers Enrique Granados and Manuel de Falla and Mexican composers Ponce and Revueltas. These concerts were often personally directed by Revueltas or Chávez, and their works were usually situated at the climax of the program as the culmination of a pan-Hispanic musical tradition (OCR, 1933b). In this way, XFX concerts extended Vasconcelos's project of hispanidad into the field of music.

In general, the Mexican art music featured in XFX programs drew predominantly from mestizo, rather than Indian, musical traditions. Although the specific works performed by Mexican composers were not always listed in XFX schedules, none of the compositions on the surviving program lists deals with explicitly indigenous themes. For example, the listings include Ponce's "Balada Mexicana," Revueltas's "8xRadio," and Chávez's "Vals Elegía" and "Antigona"—compositions much more compatible with a project of hispanidad than indigenismo (Moreno Rivas, 1989). In 1933 Chávez had not yet written his indigenous symphonies, and the compositions of Ponce and Revueltas focused almost exclusively on mestizo musical themes.

Authors of recent studies of nationalism in Mexican music have argued that, on the whole, Mexican art music never constituted a rejection of European musical styles but rather integrated elements of mestizo and indigenous music (especially melodies and rhythms) into European harmonic and symphonic structures. Composers like Ponce and Chávez specifically aimed to "dignify" and "intellectualize" popular music and adapt it to Western musical forms (Porritt, 1983; Estrada, 1984; Moreno Rivas, 1989). The art music broadcasts of XFX, then, represented a creative transformation of popular culture into a predominantly mestizo nationalist vision that celebrated the nobility and energy of a unified Mexican people. Chávez, in particular, "felt that with his music he could make a conscious effort to transcend all social class barriers, creating an end result which would be identified with and representative of, the entire national community" (Porritt, 1983:73). Ultimately, by cultivating a tradition of pan-Hispanic art music in which original works by Mexico's nationalist composers played a defining role, the SEP disseminated what it viewed as the ideal material for national integration—music that demonstrated how an authentic Mexican culture could make a meaningful contribution to European art and civilization.

Mexican Popular Music

Concerts labeled "popular" or "Mexican" were also featured prominently on XFX during prime-time listening hours; they made up almost 20 percent of evening musical broadcasts. The OCR used two very different styles of presenting popular music programs: an "official" musical format and a "vernacular" one. The "official" format featured mestizo and indigenous tunes performed by trained musicians and university-level orchestras. For example, one concert series, the *Acercamiento nacional por la educación* (*National Coming Together for Education*) was transmitted directly from various states in the republic as part of official ceremonies honoring the educational achievements of these states. The concerts were intended to popularize mestizo and indigenous music from each state in order to build what OCR officials characterized as a "strengthening panorama" of national life (OCR, 1933f:9–10). Through such musical "panoramas" XFX broadcasters highlighted and celebrated the authentic music of individual states while mapping these regional cultures onto the national domain.

These "official" concerts transformed popular regional music by assimilating popular songs to a bourgeois musical format. Andrew Goodwin argues that the key distinction between "high" and popular music is the amount of cultural status and education necessary to listen to and enjoy it. By bringing in trained musicians and orchestras to perform popular music, then, XFX's musical directors literally "invested" the music with cultural capital and thereby transformed it into a bourgeois musical form (Goodwin, 1991). In addition, the popular music collected in these programs was typically not music that dealt with politically charged or controversial themes. That is, instead of focusing on ballads (*corridos*) that charted the history of Mexico's social conflicts, political treacheries, and labor battles, these programs emphasized songs like "Linda Morena" and "Ojos Tapatíos"—songs that dwelt on the idyllic beauty of the countryside, the "joy of living," and the "love of peasant women" (OCR, 1933g; Yáñez, 1933a; Vaughan, 1982). As an accompaniment for government ceremonies, this official popular music expressed a nationalist discourse that focused on rural beauty and harmony rather than political and social conflicts.

The "vernacular" musical format broadcast by station XFX presented popular music in more or less its original form; that is, performed by regional conjuntos or instrumentalists rather than institutionally trained orchestras and musicians. One program by musicians from the states of Jalisco and Michoacán offered traditional mariachi music that XFX directors claimed was "completely unknown in the city" (OCR, 1933d). In general, these programs went to great pains to present popular music as a kind of "authentic" specimen of Mexico's ethnic roots—more like a museum piece than a part of a living musical culture. For example, Mexican Indian and regional music was grouped with other folk music of the world in a program called *International Popular Music* (OCR, 1933a). In this program, music was interspersed with expert commentary that explained the history and characteristics of the music. This commentary was specifically designed to teach Mexico City's privileged classes how to overcome their presumed discomfort with popular culture and learn to appreciate Mexico's popular arts. A publicity piece for a program of aboriginal music, for example, advertised that the broadcast would "offer all cultured people who worry about the expressions of our vernacular art, the best opportunity to appreciate the rich and varied nuances of the panorama of our national folklore" (OCR, 1933e). By decontextualizing popular music, XFX broadcasts allowed urban listeners to "appreciate" it through a disinterested, bourgeois perspective.

In addition to the *International Popular Music* program, "vernacular" music was also presented in a series of programs on Mexican musical history that ranged from the colonial period to the present. One program of nineteenth-century popular music that traced "the Mexican song [*canción*] through the years of intense revolutionary life" described the numerous political conflicts of the nineteenth century as early "revolutionary" struggles for a modern Mexican nation. According to this program, popular music was the key to understanding the "evolutionary process" of Mexican history by revealing the spirit and character of the Mexican people that propelled the republic toward its national destiny (OCR, 1933c).

Ogren highlights a similar evolutionary view of popular culture in her discussion of black nationalist discourse. For intellectuals like DuBois, she argues, "music especially offered fertile possibilities for tracing the evolution of a larger African and oral folk culture into the many forms of black creativity under slavery and afterwards" (Ogren, 1989:119). By providing a means of tracing the evolution of a unique mestizo creativity from an authentic, premodern past to the present of a dawning mestizo civilization, popular music provided SEP intellectuals with a means of bridging the divide between authenticity and civilization in their own bourgeois nationalist discourse.

Audience Reactions

Despite the careful construction of musical programming by OCR officials, the question of how Mexican audiences received and interpreted the musical nationalism of station XFX remains difficult to answer. One important source of information on rural listeners' reactions to XFX broadcasts is a collection of reports made by Luis F. Rodríguez Lomelí, an inspector for the Department of Rural Instruction. During the spring and summer of 1933, Rodríguez Lomelí carried out detailed inspections of rural schools in the central region that had received radio sets from the SEP. Inspection reports for the states of Mexico, Puebla, Tlaxcala, and Hidalgo describe how the radios were used in the schools and by the communities at large. The seventy-five donated radios were relatively inexpensive Atwater Kent receivers that operated on AC electricity. Before distribution, the radios' tuners had been set to receive only the XFX signal and locked to prevent tampering. In this way SEP officials hoped to ensure that the donated radios were used only for the government's intended pedagogical and cultural purposes.

Rodríguez Lomelí reported that enthusiasm for the donated radios was high in rural communities regardless of the fact that several rural schools, particularly in the state of Tlaxcala, could not operate their radios because of the lack of electrification. When the inspector attempted to remove a donated radio from a Tlaxcala village that had no electricity he encountered numerous objections from the townspeople, who argued that they should be allowed to keep the radio because they hoped to get a contract with the power company in the next couple of months. In another Tlaxcala village Rodríguez Lomelí was told that the villagers had sent a member to Puebla to buy a new tube for their radio, and that they were planning to install the radio in a community social building currently under construction (Rodríguez Lomeli, 1933c).

This strong interest in the donated radios did not, however, reflect an equal interest in the SEP's radio programs. Although all of the donated radios had been preset to receive only the SEP station, Rodríguez Lomelí found that in almost every case the seals had been broken in order to unlock the radio's tuning device; radio listening was not confined to station XFX. Rodríguez Lomelí reported that when he attempted to interest Puebla community members in the SEP programs, "they informed me that they frequently get together at the school, but they do not dedicate themselves to listening to our programs" (Rodríguez Lomeli, 1933b). In Tlaxcala, too, the villagers "regularly [got] together to listen to musical numbers, talks and in general the programs of other radio stations" (Rodríguez Lomeli, 1933c:1–2). In one village in the state of Mexico the radio had been removed from the school to a local theater where campesinos congregated to listen to other stations (Rodríguez Lomeli, 1933d).

Along with this general disinterest in XFX broadcasts, Rodríguez Lomelí also encountered more active resistance. He noted one teacher's comment that the musical format of XFX would not interest rural listeners because for them the music "must be popular and the songs, rancheras, since only in that form can they attract campesinos" (Rodríguez Lomeli, 1933d). In Hidalgo the inspector found "teachers who . . . insist that the radio not be tuned exclusively to the SEP station, alleging that they find the music of Agustín Lara or something equally frivolous more interesting" (Rodríguez Lomeli, 1933a). Faced with the evident popularity of commercial radio broadcasts among rural peasants, Rodríguez Lomelí could only conclude that the "mystifying spirit" (*espíritu mixtificador*) of the teachers was "filtering into the rural communities" (Rodríguez Lomeli, 1933a). Although the inspector's first instinct was to identify the teachers as the source of this resistance, the campesinos' general activism concerning their radios suggests that perhaps the teachers were not the only ones enchanted by the music of Lara and other commercially popular musicians.

Throughout his reports Rodríguez Lomelí focused on means of increasing rural listeners' interest in the SEP station. He noted, for example, that XFX broadcasts were poorly timed to the patterns of rural life and recommended that programs aimed at campesinos be shifted to evening hours (after 8:00 P.M.) or Sundays when rural workers had time to listen (Ramírez, 1933; Yáñez, 1933b). Rodríguez Lomelí reported that Puebla villagers were interested in radio programs on animal care and agriculture, health and hygiene, and "stories [*relatos*] of regional history" (Rodríguez Lomeli, 1933b). Although these program preferences may reflect considerable "filtering" by the inspector, the degree to which they emphasize local and regional interests over national ones is notable. Overall, Rodríguez Lomelí's reports suggest that for a variety of reasons the content of art music, education, and official culture that constituted the bulk of XFX broadcasts was of little interest to rural listeners.

Unlike the rural audience, which we can only learn about secondhand, XFX kept much closer contact with its Mexico City audience through radio offers that inspired numerous response letters and phone calls from listeners. A small group of twenty-five fan letters that survives in the SEP archive's radio collection provides access to the direct, personal expressions of some of Mexico City's literate radio-listening residents. These letters were written in response to a request for letters made during an *International Popular Music* program of music from the state of Michoacán which featured mestizo jarabes and danzas along with songs sung in the indigenous Tarascan dialect. While some listeners wrote to XFX simply to express their thanks and offer congratulations on the program, most wrote for the purpose of receiving a free booklet that was offered during the broadcast. Almost a third of the letters also included thoughtful expressions and reflections on the larger cultural and personal impact of the SEP's musical broadcasts (see Figure 4.2).

These letters comment on the way that XFX broadcasts built a common knowledge of a unified Mexican musical tradition and allowed individual listeners to experience the national panorama so carefully constructed by OCR officials. One listener wrote to thank the station for a musical broadcast that "spiritually transported" him to his native region (OCR, 1933h). Another listener congratulated the station for "making known the regional music of all parts of the Republic, and in this way touching the sentiments of everyone who more or less relive the memory of their hours of youth upon hearing the sounds of regional music, of country music that to some is bound to be so familiar." He continued by saying that "one must imagine that here [in Mexico City] there are peoples from all parts of the Republic and that each one will remember his native region upon listening to these village songs" (OCR, 1933h). As a group, the letters suggest that some literate urban listeners interpreted the popular musical broadcasts of XFX as building a shared nostalgia with other Mexicans and generating a feeling of sympathy and community at the national level. Although this nostalgia was based on the listeners' individual childhood memories of different regions and states (that were further distinguished and differentiated in XFX musi-

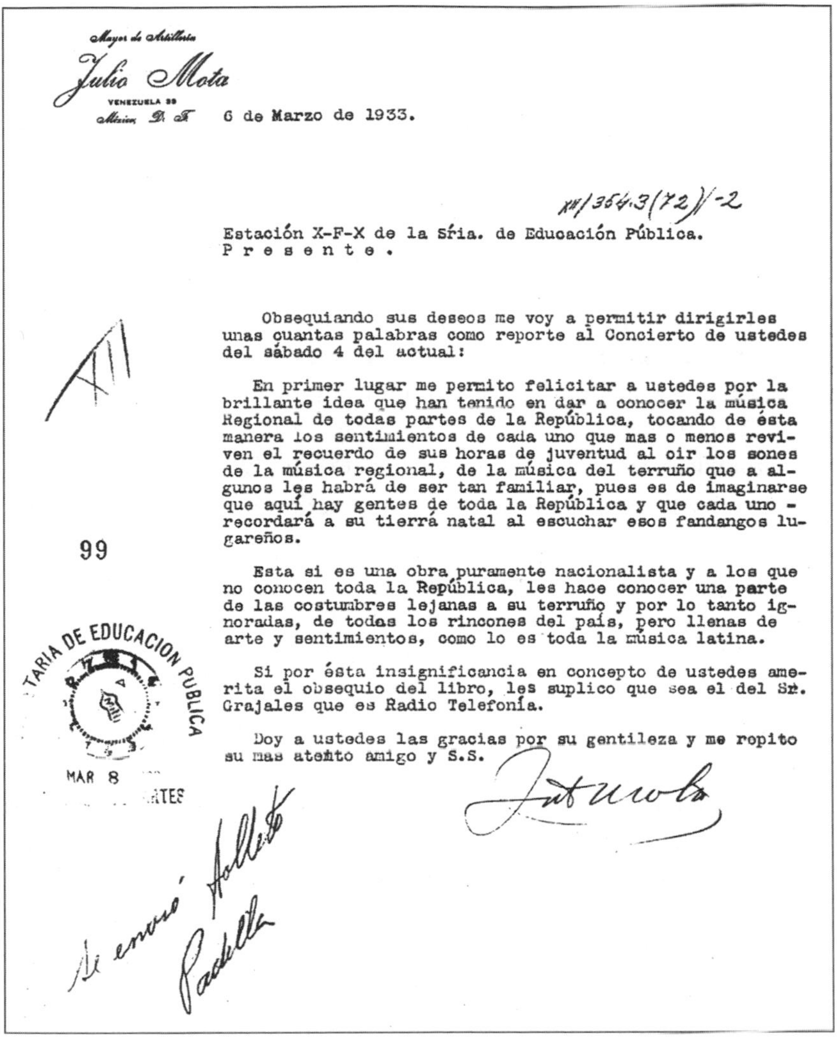

Mayor de Artillería

Julio Mota

VENEZUELA 99

México, D. F. 6 de Marzo de 1933.

xx/364.3(72)/-2

Estación X-F-X de la Sría. de Educación Pública.
P r e s e n t e .

    Obsequiando sus deseos me voy a permitir dirigirles
unas cuantas palabras como reporte al Concierto de ustedes
del sábado 4 del actual:

    En primer lugar me permito felicitar a ustedes por la
brillante idea que han tenido en dar a conocer la música
Regional de todas partes de la República, tocando de ésta
manera los sentimientos de cada uno que mas o menos revi-
ven el recuerdo de sus horas de juventud al oir los sones
de la música regional, de la música del terruño que a al-
gunos les habrá de ser tan familiar, pues es de imaginarse
que aquí hay gentes de toda la República y que cada uno -
recordará a su tierra natal al escuchar esos fandangos lu-
gareños.

    Esta si es una obra puramente nacionalista y a los que
no conocen toda la República, les hace conocer una parte
de las costumbres lejanas a su terruño y por lo tanto ig-
noradas, de todos los rincones del país, pero llenas de
arte y sentimientos, como lo es toda la música latina.

    Si por ésta insignificancia en concepto de ustedes ame-
rita el obsequio del libro, les suplico que sea el del Sr.
Grajales que es Radio Telefonía.

    Doy a ustedes las gracias por su gentileza y me repito
su mas atento amigo y S.S.

Figure 4.2 A listener response letter sent to station XFX, March 6, 1933.
(Oficina Cultural Radiotelefónica, Reportes, expediente 33, caja 1315; Archivo
Histórico de la Secretaría de Educación Pública, Mexico City.)

cal programs), it could be recognized as "Mexican" and shared in common through the simultaneity of the radio medium.

The activities of station XFX between 1929 and 1934 played a significant part in the Mexican government's efforts to use the broadcasting medium to assert a strong political and cultural presence in Mexican civil society. At the same time that Mexico's ruling party was institutionalizing its political power and expanding its bureaucratic structures, it became increasingly active in radio broadcasting. The Education Ministry's station was the first major testing ground for state-sponsored cultural broadcasts, which would expand greatly under the Cárdenas administration in 1936 with the founding of the DAPP. This department would take over where the SEP's Office of Cultural Radiotelephony left off and produce the *National Hour* program with a nationalistic musical content similar to the one originally developed on station XFX (Norris, 1962). With the *National Hour*, which all Mexican stations are still required to transmit every Sunday night, state-sponsored nationalism became an institutionalized part of commercial broadcasting. Thus, although station XFX is not representative of Mexico's predominantly commercial radio system, a study of this station's policies and program content offers a window onto the state's nationalist project and the history of the broadcasting system as a whole.

As rural audience reactions to XFX broadcasts indicate, however, the most popular and lasting radio discourse of the 1930s was not the programming disseminated by government stations but the programming produced by Mexico City's dominant commercial broadcasters, especially Emilio Azcárraga. The significance of government broadcasting for Mexican radio as a whole, then, was a function not of its direct impact on radio audiences, but of its role as an influential model of radio programming that was particularly audible (rather than visible) to commercial broadcasters. Over the course of the decade the Mexican state combined its own broadcasting ventures with increased control over the content of commercial broadcasting stations in order to effectively reach the public with its official nationalist vision.

Nation as Market

As the response to station XFX discussed in Chapter 4 indicates, the radio programs that captured the popular imagination were not those produced by government broadcasters, but commercial programs coming primarily from Mexico City stations. Commercial radio in Mexico was shaped in part by state activism and in part by the dependent development of the Mexican radio industry. Under these pressures, broadcasters created a distinctly nationalist idiom for the commercial radio market. In this chapter I explore this "market nationalism" through a structural analysis of the broadcasting system and a content analysis of prime-time radio programming.

The Context of State Activism

To understand the period of intensified government involvement in radio broadcasting between about 1936 and 1939, it is necessary first to situate state activism in the context of the political economy of the Cárdenas years. After coming to power in 1934, Lázaro Cárdenas broke the extra-legal power established by Calles, exiled the former president, and began a series of reformist political projects. These included the redistribution of land to peasant farming cooperatives (*ejidos*), the encouragement of worker unionization and political organization, deficit spending for economic and social programs, and the reorganization of the Partido Nacional Revolucionario (Haber, 1989; Skidmore and Smith, 1997). The federal government legitimated this new wave of activism—from land redistribution to the oil expropriation of 1938—by presenting it as an expression of revolutionary nationalism, an ideology that positioned the state as the natural and inevitable executor of the egalitarian principles of the Revolution and equated state intervention with national values and interests (Hamilton, 1982; Vázquez and Meyer, 1985).

As Alan Knight cautions, however, the economic nationalism of the Cárdenas era must be seen in its international as well as its national context (Knight, 1985). The worldwide economic depression, for example, shielded Mexico's nationalist policies from international intervention. Hamilton argues that Latin American nationalism rarely met strong opposition from dominant countries during the 1930s because those countries were preoccupied with their own economic problems (Hamilton, 1982). The 1930s was also a period when U.S. corporations increasingly thought of Latin America as a market for their goods rather than solely a source of raw materials. This meant that military intervention and the fostering of political instability were viewed somewhat less favorably by the United States as a means of dealing with Latin American countries. In fact, the Roosevelt administration supported the Cárdenas government's nationalistic policies "as a means of increasing purchasing power and converting Mexico into a stable client of the United States" (Fejes, 1986:25).

World political developments also promoted international tolerance of Mexican nationalism. With the rise of German and Italian expansionism in Europe and Japanese expansionism in Asia, the United States felt the need to create an inter-American alliance to protect the hemisphere from these encroaching influences. Rather than follow a "Big Stick" policy that might provoke resentment and leave Latin America open to fascist influence, Roosevelt initiated the Good Neighbor Policy. The United States renounced its earlier claim that it had the right to intervene militarily in any Latin American country and opened new channels of exchange and communication. The Good Neighbor Policy reduced the U.S. government's dependence on force as a mode of intervention in Latin America and relied instead on North American economic and cultural expansion in the region. As Fred Fejes argues, the policy did not represent a liquidation of past expansionist goals, but rather a creative transformation of the methods of control and domination. For example, U.S. corporate influence over advertising and the mass media became a key means of economic domination. On the other hand, countries such as Mexico were able to take advantage of the new political objectives and conciliatory strategies of the United States to achieve their own nationalistic goals. Cárdenas, for example, coupled his nationalistic politics with a militant antifascism that "fitted perfectly with Roosevelt's hemispheric and world strategies" (Fejes, 1986:25). In this context, the U.S. government had difficulty opposing the progressive and nationalistic policies of his administration.

These progressive policies did not aim to overturn Mexico's capitalist economy. Rather, in the face of international instability and continuing U.S. expansionism, the Cárdenas administration used nationalistic policies to reorganize the economy in the interest of a more even process of national development that benefited workers and peasants along with capital and business. By helping to stabilize and rationalize the economy and improve the purchasing power of laborers, the Cárdenas reforms actually helped to create the conditions for capital accumulation and industrial expansion. These reforms failed, however, to disrupt the long tradition of government aid to privileged sectors of the dominant classes in the form of contract favoritism, economic protectionism, and the encouragement of industrial cartels (Hamilton, 1982; Leal, 1986; Haber 1989).

Along with economic stabilization, the Cárdenas government promoted social stability through the formation of a corporatist system of political and social representation that increased state autonomy in the coordination and integration of competing social groups. In 1938 the official party reorganized along corporatist lines (borrowed from the political systems of Italy, Spain, and Portugal), creating four representative groups: the agricultural (peasant) sector, the labor sector, the military sector, and the popular (middle-class) sector. This system of representation not only created institutional barriers to a worker-peasant coalition, it also greatly enhanced the state's ability to coordinate the different social sectors and maintain political control. Although the Cárdenas administration won real benefits for workers and peasants, it also established a "corporatist form of authoritarianism" that protected the hegemony of the official party and the stability of the capitalist social system while appearing to create a populist and inclusive political process (Reyna and Weinert, 1977:xiii; Hamilton, 1982; Skidmore and Smith, 1997).

State Broadcasting Activities

During this period of economic reform and political reorganization, the state greatly expanded its role in broadcasting as a means of increasing its presence and influence in civil society and building mass consensus for government actions. Mexican government leaders recognized the power of radio broadcasting to build national identity and unity. In 1937 the secretary of communications and transport complained that "almost nine tenths of the country is without adequate communications and millions of people . . . still cannot be incorporated into our national life" (Norris, 1962:27). Radio, with its unique ability to transmit across great distances in a format that was particularly well suited to Mexico's highly oral culture, promised to establish communication with these "lost" citizens. Although Cárdenas, like his predecessors, left the development of radio largely in the hands of commercial broadcasting entrepreneurs, his administration took significant steps to guide and shape that development.

One arena of increased government activity was the regulatory framework of broadcasting. The Cárdenas government used regulatory controls to increase the presence of official state voices over private radio stations and strengthen the nationalistic orientation of the broadcasting system as a whole. In 1936, Cárdenas created the Autonomous Department of Press and Publicity (DAPP), which gave his administration centralized regulatory control over the content of most of Mexico's communication media, including radio broadcasting, newspapers, films, books, magazines, and the theater (Barbour, 1940; Mejía Barquera, 1989). A 1937 article from the *New York Times* titled "1,100 Propagandists in a Mexican Bureau" described the DAPP as a phenomenal success in the eyes of the Mexican state. Not only did the new agency provide a central clearing house for government information, it also "eliminate[d] much reporting by supplying a daily flood of information" to all media outlets.

The Cárdenas administration also reformed the Mexican communication laws in 1936 under the title "Regulations for Commercial, Experimental, Cultural and Amateur Broadcasting Stations." This law increased the amount of government programming time required on all commercial and noncommercial (cultural) stations from ten to thirty minutes per day and demanded that all stations include at least 25 percent "typical

Mexican music" in each radio program. Like earlier laws, the 1936 radio law prohibited the transmission of political messages over the radio (Barbour, 1940; Arredondo Ramírez and Sánchez Ruíz, 1986; Mejía Barquera, 1989). When several powerful broadcasters protested the law requiring a fixed percentage of "typical Mexican music" in every program and suggested that they be given more flexibility in presenting music of Mexican authorship, their petition was denied. The secretary of communications and transport responded that such a change would destroy the specific aim of the law, which was "none other than that of diffusing our typical music with greater intensity, as this constitutes one of the most fertile manifestations of our popular art" (Barbour, 1940:101).

The state also expanded its own broadcasting activities. Although government radio had been nationally oriented since the 1920s, Philip L. Barbour argues that the Mexican state did not begin a concerted and coordinated plan to use radio broadcasting to address a national audience until 1937. Through its radio station, XEDP, the DAPP initiated a large number of propaganda and entertainment programs. One of the DAPP's most ambitious efforts was the *National Hour*, a one-hour weekly program that made its debut in July 1937. The program was transmitted from station XEDP and broadcast over commercial station XEW's powerful long-wave and shortwave transmitters. By law, every station in the country technically capable of rebroadcasting the program was required to do so. By this means the state put together a national "network" of stations to broadcast the program.

The content of the *National Hour* offers a glimpse into the ways the state promoted and disseminated its version of a Mexican national culture. The weekly programs were composed of cultural and educational features, including Mexican popular and classical music, documentary dramas of Mexican history, and poetry readings, interspersed with government announcements and progress reports. Government reports included presidential speeches, information on the national census, and discussions of the petroleum expropriation and nationalization. According to Renfro C. Norris, the programs focused on government efforts "to carry out the social and economic aims of the Revolution" and aspired to strengthen "the sense of civic responsibility in all Mexicans" (Norris, 1962:13). Although the *National Hour* was designed as a vehicle of state propaganda, it devoted a majority of its time to conveying what one government broadcaster described as "cultural information." During the period 1937–39 government reports accounted for only about fifteen to twenty minutes of program time. The rest of the hour was filled with an array of music, drama, and history that aimed to expose a national audience to an officially sanctioned Mexican culture (Norris, 1962).

This content also indicates the continuities between the DAPP's broadcasting initiative and the XFX radio project developed a few years earlier by the SEP. As discussed in Chapter 4, key personnel from the SEP radio project went to work for the DAPP and the *National Hour* program. Not surprisingly, the *National Hour* continued the SEP's emphasis on art music, with a focus on Mexican composers and popular cultural themes. For example, the program for October 10, 1937, highlighted the composition "Danzas Mayas," written and directed by Efrain Pérez and performed by the Orquesta Sinfónica DAPP (see Figure 5.1). As this and other examples indicate, the content of the *National Hour* and other DAPP programs drew liberally on the model of a "national musical panorama" developed by broadcasters at station XFX.

The Azcárraga Group and the Benefits of Market Nationalism

Over the course of the decade, state broadcasting activities sent a clear signal to commercial broadcasters: maintain the favorable opinion of the central government by promoting "typical Mexican music" and avoiding political and religious discourse. While the good favor of the central state may not have been essential for most radio stations, it was quite important to a large broadcaster aiming to corner the national market. As mentioned earlier, Mexico's lopsided model of development was predicated, in part, on close state-industry relations. As Stephen Haber convincingly argues, the state used its powers to limit competition and aid the growth of monopolies and oligopolies in many industries (Haber, 1989).

Such was clearly the case with Emilio Azcárraga and his XEW-led broadcasting empire. By 1938 Azcárraga controlled two national networks loosely affiliated with NBC (XEW) and CBS (XEQ). In 1941 he entered a partnership with Clemente Serna Martínez, owner of Monterrey's most important radio station, and created Radio Programas de México (RPM) to manage his radio empire. By 1942 RPM had sixty Mexican affiliates

Figure 5.1 A program schedule for the *National Hour* (*Excelsior* [Mexico City], October 9, 1937, p. 8.)

—almost half of all radio stations in Mexico (Arredondo Ramírez and Sánchez Ruíz, 1986). By 1945 RPM had established a regional presence, distributing programs to thirty-eight affiliates in Costa Rica, Colombia, Ecuador, El Salvador, Peru, Honduras, Nicaragua, Panama, the Dominican Republic, Uruguay, and Venezuela (Baer, 1991).

In explaining the particular orientation of Azcárraga's radio activities, Miriam D. Baer discounts the impact of state broadcasting policies and instead emphasizes the commercial policies of NBC. According to Baer, Azcárraga learned two things from NBC: the need for national coverage and the need for a "national media image" (Baer, 1991:58). This seems to beg the question, however, of why Azcárraga chose the particular national image that he did; that is, one that emphasized a unique content of Mexican popular music and a distinctly Mexican cultural orientation. As XEW's owner himself put it in a 1943 interview: "Indeed, this is an eminently Mexican radio station!" (¡Y eso sí, esta es una radiodifusora eminemente mexicana!)(Leyva, 1992:136).

To the extent that Azcárraga's nationalistic orientation was a commercial strategy, it was probably a response to his position as an intermediary for North American media corporations. By designing and delivering a unique content for the Mexican market, Azcárraga was no longer an easily replaceable middleman dependent on North American producers, but an indispensable provider of a unique commodity: commercial Mexican broadcasting. Azcárraga created a demand that he alone could satisfy. This worked particularly well for the Azcárraga Group as it developed parallel enterprises in the recording and film industries. The role of film stars in the recording and radio arenas, and vice versa, provided the critical mass of talent to support a marketplace vision of national culture. Perhaps the best way to account for the particular path chosen by the Azcárraga Group is through a combination of state and market forces: the state's direct and indirect interests in the broadcasting field established the nationalistic conditions under which Azcárraga's unique marketing strategy could flourish.

Commercial Radio Content

How did market nationalism manifest itself in the content of Mexico City radio stations? How did Mexican radio content differ from U.S. radio content, for example? Printed radio program schedules and compilations of popular songs provide a useful means of evaluating the types of programs that dominated the evening broadcasting hours. Although these listings offer limited information about certain aspects of radio music (orchestration, melody, and lyrics), they give a comprehensive view of radio content—including performers, program formats, and musical styles—that has not been examined by previous scholars. I analyzed XEW program listings that appeared in the newspaper *Excelsior* during two periods: October 1937 through March 1938, and October 1938 through March 1939. Two weekdays and two weekend days were selected at random from each month within these periods, making a total of twenty-four daily listings for each six-month period. Only programs airing during the evening hours of 8:00–11:00 P.M. were examined, totaling 144 programming hours for the period between 1937 and 1939.

In contrast to the formats of most North American network affiliates, which featured dramatic and comedic programs during these hours (with some musical programs appearing in the late evening hours), the vast majority of XEW prime-time features were musical programs. On weeknights, 92 percent of programming time was devoted to musical features, and on weekend nights, when the *National Hour* contributed more nonmusical content than normal, 70 percent of broadcast time was filled by exclusively musical programs. Moreover, none of the programs broadcast by XEW was from the United States, and only one was explicitly foreign in origin, namely a performance by an Argentinean group. Despite XEW's links with NBC, no U.S. dramatic programs were rebroadcast in the prime evening hours. This clearly indicates that Azcárraga's affiliations with North American networks had little if any direct influence over his prime-time schedule. Instead, music reigned supreme.

Musical programming dominated the evening hours on other stations as well. A sample of evening schedules for station XEB from 1938 to 1948 culled from the Mexico City newspaper *El Universal* shows the percentage of programming time devoted to music (see Figure 5.2).[1] Station XEB, owned by the Buen Tono cigarette company, was one of Mexico's first stations, and during the 1930s and 1940s it was still one of the top two or three most popular stations in Mexico City (Sydney Ross, 1942). As Figure 5.2 illustrates, music represented almost 90 percent of evening programming

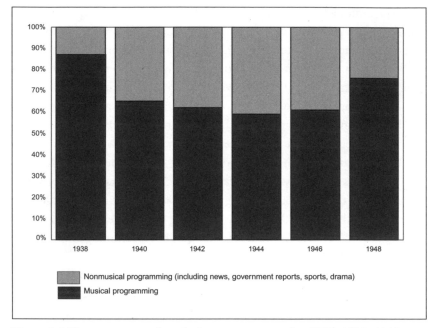

Figure 5.2 The percentage of musical programs on station XEB, 1938–1948. (From data compiled from station XEB, XEX, and Radio Mil program schedules printed in *El Universal* [Mexico City].)

on XEB in 1938. Although the percentage of music fell to a low of less than 60 percent in 1944, by 1948 it was once again at more than 75 percent. In large part, the drop in musical programming during 1940–46 can be explained by the increase of news, government reports, and propaganda programs during the World War II years. However, there was also an increase in the presence of dramatic programs, game shows, and sports broadcasts over the course of the 1940s. Although musical programs returned to their dominant position in the years after the war, the percentage of news and other nonmusical programs did not drop to its prewar level, but remained a significant component of the evening schedule.

Returning to the 1937–39 sample of XEW programs, it is evident that a particular type of musical performance dominated evening broadcasts. According to the evening schedules, Mexican orchestras (*orquestas*) — often conducted by such well-known Mexican composers as Tata Nacho and

Alfonso Esparza Oteo—made up 82 percent of all musical programs on weekdays and 71 percent on weekends. The roots of the Mexican orquesta can be traced back to nineteenth-century *orquestas típicas*: "typical" folk ensembles consisting of violins, psaltery, guitar, mandolins, and contrabass. The first orquesta típica was the Orquesta Típica Mexicana founded in 1884 by the National Conservatory of Music. Manuel Peña describes these orquestas as distinctly middle-class groups which, out of a spirit of patriotism (*costumbrismo*), adopted *charro* costumes and other elements of mestizo folk music and culture (Peña, 1985). Caes af Geijerstam notes that these mostly urban dance ensembles often took their repertoires from upper-class salon music, including pasadobles, polkas, and waltzes (Geijerstam, 1976).

During the 1920s and 1930s, however, the orquestas were transformed by two very different cultural developments. First, Mexican orquestas were influenced by the enormous influx of regional folk music into Mexico City in the post-revolutionary years. These influences included mariachis and *canciones* from the Bajío region; marimbas from Chiapas, Oaxaca, and Tabasco; along with corridos, huapangos, and other regional musical forms. At the same time, U.S. commercial culture was also shaping the orquestas. According to Peña (1985), trumpets, saxophones, and other brass instruments became part of the ensembles as a result of the growing influence of North American swing bands in Mexican musical culture. Moreno Rivas (1989), however, suggests that the trumpet, at least, invaded the mariachi orquesta in imitation of the Cuban style of trumpeting made famous in Mexico by the Sexteto Típico Habanero. Juan S. Garrido, a composer and orquesta leader at XEW during the 1930s, contends that Emilio Azcárraga was personally responsible for transforming the mariachi orquesta by removing the harp and adding the trumpet. According to Garrido, Azcárraga "wanted to broadcast mariachi music played by authentic Jalisco bands, but thought the sound was too thin to be reproduced by radio. . . . He therefore suggested that the melody be carried by a more piercing instrument" (Geijerstam, 1976:43). Although this claim may be exaggerated (Moreno Rivas, 1989), there is no question that the instrumentation and style of popular music were frequently altered in response to the technological requirements of early recording and broadcasting practices (Ogren, 1989).

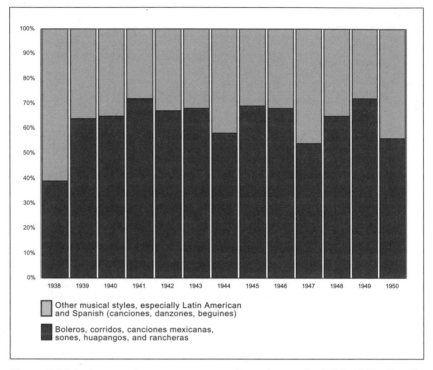

Figure 5.3 Mexican music as a percentage of popular music, 1938-1950. (Based on data from J. S. Garrido, *Historia de la música popular en México, 1896-1973* [Mexico City: Editorial Extemporaneos, 1974].)

Because radio listings rarely describe the particular songs or even the types of songs that were performed by the orquestas and their featured singers, it is helpful to look at the listings of top radio hits compiled by Garrido in his *Historia de la música popular en México*. An examination of hit songs for the years 1938-50, for which Garrido lists an average of fifty-nine songs per year, shows the predominance of Mexican music (see Figure 5.3). Among the Mexican songs he lists are *boleros, corridos, canciones mexicanas, sones, huapangos, and rancheras*. In particular, the compilation shows the rise of ranchera music during this period (see Figure 5.4). The large number of ranchera hits in the late 1940s reflects the prolific songwriting of José Alfredo Jiménez. William Grandante estimates that after Augustín Lara, Jiménez was probably Mexico's most prolific songwriter,

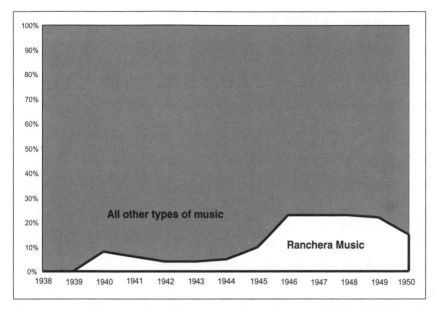

Figure 5.4 Ranchera music as a percentage of popular music, 1938–1950. (Based on data from J. S. Garrido, *Historia de la música popular en México: 1896–1973* [Mexico City: Editorial Extemporaneos, 1974].)

with more than three hundred songs published (Grandante, 1983). As discussed in Chapter 4, the commercial ranchera is an urban musical form that romanticizes pre-revolutionary social relations and idealizes the countryside. Mexico's Bajío region—comprised of Michoacán, Jalisco, Querétaro, Aguascalientes, and Gunajuato—particularly came to embody the idyllic "soul" of the nation in ranchera songs and films (Geijerstam, 1976; Mosse, 1991). Although Jiménez was an important figure in "urbanizing" the ranchera by emphasizing the working-class cantina and the *macho*'s lost love over the rancho and the countryside, the basic sentimentalism of the ranchera continued to evoke an antimodern nostalgia for a popular, paternalist utopia (Grandante, 1983:143; Moreno Rivas, 1989).

The percentage of distinctly "Mexican" radio hits rose and fell between 1938 and 1950, but it never dropped below 40 percent. The remaining hit songs rarely came from the United States or Europe (for example, blues or foxtrots), but were primarily from other Latin American countries. The Cuban rumba, mambo, and *danzón*; Brazilian samba; and Argentinean tango were among the many Latin American styles that filled the Mexican airwaves. Many of these styles were "Mexicanized" by local musicians. The clearest example is probably the Cuban bolero style, which inspired a Mexicanized bolero form that, by the 1950s, developed into a distinct ranchera-bolero hybrid that was associated most directly with the songs of Pedro Infante (Moreno Rivas, 1989).

The Dialogue of Popular Culture

This history suggests that Mexican popular music should be viewed not as an essential or authentic cultural product, but as a communicative interaction—a dialogue—between "local" and "foreign" musical practices. This is clearly the case with Agustín Lara, a successful musician who wrote hundreds of hit songs and had his own radio program—*The Blue Hour* (*La hora azul*)—on station XEW. Although Lara defined an era of Mexican cinematic and musical production, he was often criticized as a non-Mexican influence. Many of his songs celebrated Spanish themes, drew on foreign musical rhythms (especially the Cuban bolero), and achieved international acclaim. One critic describes his songs as overly commercialized and fit only for a "cosmopolitan musical atmosphere" (Stevenson, 1952). In contrast, other scholars describe Lara's music as "naturalized" and "Mexicanized" (Garrido, 1974; Moreno Rivas, 1989). Referring specifically to the Afro-Cuban bolero style so prominent on Mexican radio between 1930 and 1950, Geijerstam argues that Lara reworked the bolero "to conform to the native *canción* tradition" (Geijerstam, 1976:101–2). Adela Pineda Franco traces Lara's specific adaptations of the bolero rhythm to the urban Mexican context. She argues that Lara must ultimately be understood as having been perceived differently at different historical moments—at one time a modern, bohemian artist; at another a conservative pillar of Mexican tradition (Pineda Franco, 1996).

As this perspective suggests, popular music takes on meaning only under the particular historical conditions in which it is enacted as a tradition, trend, or art. Only voices that are historically grounded, physically embodied, and socially intentioned can participate in the cultural dialogues that shape popular musical practice (Bakhtin, 1995, 1997). Thus, scholars can interpret popular music only through the institutions and actors who attempt to articulate it and mobilize it for particular ends. This under-standing of culture *as communication* resonates with approaches developed by a variety of cultural historians and applied to Latin American popular culture (Isaac, 1982; Susman, 1984; Beezley, Martin, and French, 1994). Indeed, the concept of popular culture as dialogue provides a sense of his-torical grounding and political specificity that is lacking in recent theories designed to capture the dynamics of popular culture — theories of transcul-turation, creolization, and hybridity (Pérez Montfort, 1994; García Can-clini, 1995; Trigo, 1996). While these theories tend to become abstract and depoliticized (Chen, 1996), a historical understanding of popular culture as communicative practice attempts to keep both cultural expression and political intention in play in order to capture the flow, or dialogue, of cul-tural interaction.

The Triumph of Market Nationalism

The year 1939 marked a significant shift in the political economy of Mexi-can broadcasting as the federal government closed the DAPP, ended its coordinated plan of state broadcasting, and commercialized the content of its official party station, XEFO. Government broadcasting stations de-clined from a peak of fourteen to only eight in 1939 (Arredondo Ramírez and Sánchez Ruíz, 1986). Nationalistic regulations remained, but were lim-ited. These limits can be clearly seen in the government's attempt to revise the Law of General Means of Communication (LVGC). Beginning in the mid-1930s, General Francisco Mújica, a close Cárdenas adviser and the secretary of communications and transport, spearheaded a major revision of the 1932 LVGC. Initially, Mújica proposed the creation of a national network of government broadcasting stations financed by a European-style subscription system. Faced with strong protests from commercial broad-casters and allied commercial interests, however, Mújica was forced to modify his plan. By the time his proposal reached the Cámara de Diputa-dos in 1937, it had been reduced to a proposal for a federal commission to regulate commercial broadcasting and a tax on radio receivers to help support cultural stations. After even more industry lobbying, the LVGC that emerged from the Cámara in 1939 was actually quite favorable to commercial interests. The law directly benefited the broadcasting industry by removing import duties on radio parts and equipment. In addition, the Radio Advisory Committee (Comisión Consultiva de Radio), originally designed as a committee to investigate the problems of commercial broadcasting, became a means of industry influence over the regulatory process (Mejía Barquera, 1989).

When the state seemed to threaten the commercial model of broadcasting, the radio industry consolidated its organization and flexed its collective muscles. In 1937 a group of powerful regional broadcasters formed the Mexican Association of Radio Broadcasting Stations in order to improve their representation in the capital. Mexico City broadcasters soon gained control of the organization, however, and the name was changed to Mexican Association of Commercial Radio Broadcasting Stations (Asociación Mexicana de Estaciones Radiodifusoras Comerciales, or AMERC). AMERC became a powerful lobbying organization for the industry and was the main force behind the establishment, in 1942, of the National Chamber of the Radio Industry (Cámara Nacional de la Industria de la Radiodifusión, or CIR, later CIRT). The CIR gave commercial broadcasters a national profile as well as an institutional springboard from which to influence both national and international broadcasting policy (see Chapter 7).

After 1939, Mexico's leaders were happy to leave radio broadcasting primarily in private hands as long as these broadcasters were willing to preserve the political hegemony of the Mexican state. As Fernando Mejía-Barquera has observed, with the resurgence of political conservatism in the final year of the Cárdenas administration, the government moved to a new broadcasting policy that relied on a sense of " 'cordiality' and 'confidence' that [commercial broadcasters] would collaborate with the state when and if they were asked" (Mejía Barquera, 1989:93). An example of this new relationship of "cordial collaboration" can be seen in the case of the *National Hour*. After the DAPP closed in 1939, the program came under the auspices of the Ministry of the Interior (Gobernación). However, no new government station was launched to distribute the program. Instead, the *National Hour* was produced in the XEW studios under commercial supervision — under Emilio Azcárraga's wing, as it were. Azcárraga became the quasi-official representative of the "national interests" of Mexican broadcasting beginning in the late 1930s. The Azcárraga Group's unique national role, however, cannot be understood outside the broader context of government activism. By mandating a nationalistic broadcasting content of Mexican popular music during the formative years of radio development, the state played a significant role in promoting a "golden age" of Mexican commercial music during the 1930s and 1940s.

The Paternal Voice of the Nation

In radio broadcasting as in other aspects of cultural and political life, paternalism solved many problems for the post-revolutionary state. In the era of the "Jefe Máximo" and "Tata Lázaro,"[1] paternalism legitimized and naturalized the newly acquired power of the revolutionary government. I use *paternalism* here to mean a system of social power relations based on a model of male control over, and responsibility for, both male and female dependents. Paternalism was based on the figure of the patriarch, who provided an integrated field of social authority encompassing moral guidance, economic control, and political allegiance. Images of macho heroes —leaders who could demand filial respect of men and sexual privileges of women— dominated state-sponsored monuments, ceremonies, and festivals during the 1930s. They also dominated Mexican commercial culture. In particular, the ubiquitous *comedia ranchera* genre, with its pre-revolutionary images of rural haciendas, *patrones*, and *peones*, filled cinema, theater, popular music, and radio with visions of paternalistic authority (Mora, 1982; O'Malley, 1986; Pérez Montfort, 1994).

Ilene V. O'Malley's study of hero cults and the Mexican state provides an especially clear interpretation of why and how paternalism became such a central cultural discourse during the 1930s. She argues that the state used the relatively depoliticized values of virility, machismo, and paternalism to replace the threatening political and class aspects of revolutionary heroes such as Emiliano Zapata and Francisco Villa. Zapata, for example, was officially inducted as a "national hero" in 1931. In commemoration, his remains were placed in a crypt in Cuatla, Morelos, the following year and crowned with a statue of Zapata on horseback "looking down to and placing a hand on the shoulder of a simple campesino, who looked up to him in admiration" (O'Malley, 1986:60). This official icon worked to transform Zapata from a representative of campesino interests into a respectable (read bourgeois) leader who could interpret and guide peasant interests from a more lofty position (that of the central state). As Samuel Brunk points out, the official Zapata "did not have to convince everyone at all times"; it only had to distract and disrupt the formation of more radical interpretations and uses of the Zapata image (Brunk, 1998:487).

In comparison with official ceremonies and statues, radio offered the state a dynamic and flexible medium with which to elaborate paternalist discourse on a national scale. In particular, the state used radio to evoke the nation through a single paternal voice: the voice of the Mexican president. Presidential radio use during the 1930s reveals two broad modes of paternalist discourse: a strategy of calming the public via radio and a strategy of rallying the public through a radio rallying call (*grito*) modeled on the independence grito of Padre Hidalgo. The broadcasting activities of Lázaro Cárdenas, who worked to institutionalize radio as a medium of communication between the president and the people, are especially illustrative of this strategy.

Radio and the Mexican Presidency

Although Mexican presidents had been speaking occasionally on the radio since the mid-1920s, the practice did not become a frequent and regular part of the presidency until the Calles and Cárdenas administrations of the 1930s. As discussed earlier, radio use was part of a broader institutionalization of the post-revolutionary state that took place through the organization of the official party (the PNR) and the proliferation of central government bureaucracy. The founding of the PNR newspaper, *El Nacional*, was followed closely by the founding of a PNR radio station, XEFO, in 1931. Station XEFO soon became a primary outlet for presidential broadcasting. As Mexican presidents took to the airwaves more frequently, their use of radio began to follow a distinct pattern. Along with annual and commemorative addresses and reports to the nation, presidential broadcasts fell into two broad categories: electronic sedatives (*sedativos electrónicos*) and electronic rallying calls (*gritos electrónicos*). In both cases, these radio speeches had a dual function as communication and action. That is, the speeches constituted political action in and of themselves, in the same way that a declaration of war is both an action (the war is begun) and a communication about that action (the war is announced). The modality of communication—in this case radio broadcasting—put a particular imprint on both what was being done and what was being said. The speeches became newsworthy political events in themselves with anticipated material consequences, in part because of the perceived power of radio as a medium of mass communication.

Sedativos Electrónicos

Whether or not radio actually had the direct and powerful effect of a "mass sedative," the social discourse surrounding radio during the 1930s most often assumed that it did. This assumption shaped both the way radio was used by public officials and the way radio "effects" were identified in public discourse. A classic example of this from North American radio was the first "Fireside Chat" broadcast made by U.S. president Franklin Roosevelt in March 1933. In the depths of the economic depression and in the face of an imminent banking crisis, the speech aimed to renew public faith in the central government and the economic system. Indeed, the speech succeeded in "saving capitalism" (according to contemporaries) by encouraging millions of Americans to redeposit their savings in private financial institutions (Hayes, 1993b). In the hands of a talented speaker, radio had the ability to calm public fears in times of crisis and upheaval.

Public discourse on presidential radio broadcasting in Mexico reveals a similar understanding of the power of radio. In February 1930, Mexico's president, Pascual Ortiz Rubio, made a national radio broadcast shortly after recuperating from an assassination attempt. Afterward, the *New York Times* reported that Ortiz Rubio "spoke over the radio last night and his speech had the double effect of reassuring the country as to his recovery from an assassin's bullet and as to the constructive policy that he plans to adopt" (*New York Times*, 1930:6). According to the article, the Mexican public viewed Ortiz Rubio's speech as a generous and brave act in the wake of the Inauguration Day attempt on his life. While stabilizing the domestic sphere, the speech was also described as strengthening Mexico's image abroad by "calming" foreign exchange and buoying the peso. The act of instantaneous mass communication by the president signaled the stability and order of the body politic.

President Cárdenas also used radio to invoke order and stability during his tumultuous administration. Specifically, he turned to radio during three major regime crises: the Calles crisis, the Cedillo Rebellion, and the aftermath of the oil nationalization. Even before taking office Cárdenas was faced with the problem of what to do with former president Calles—Jefe Máximo of the Revolution—who had become Mexico's de facto ruler and the power behind the presidency. Although Cárdenas denounced Calles in his New Year's radio address of 1935, his critical strike came in June 1935 when he purged his cabinet of Calles supporters and politically isolated his former mentor (Mejía Barquera, 1989; Krauze, 1997b). At this politically sensitive moment, Cárdenas gave a major radio address to the Rotary International Club meeting in Mexico City. In this speech, carried by stations XEFO and XEW, Cárdenas assured both the nation and the international community of the government's "legalism and institutional stability." He pointedly observed that Mexico was happy to welcome the Rotary Club into the heart of the capital "because we have no situations to hide from them, nor reasons to be ashamed in front of the world" (Cárdenas, 1940:21). As a PNR publication proclaimed years later, "General Cárdenas was demonstrating to the world, with the serene solution that he gave to the political crisis promoted by Calles and his associates, that Mexico was now a country of adult institutions" (Cárdenas, 1940:20). In the language of the day, radio offered Cárdenas a means to soothe and pacify both domestic and foreign worries over the stability of his regime. As with Ortiz Rubio, radio gave Cárdenas a medium through which to extend and strengthen himself as the voice of paternal authority.

The greatest crisis of the Cárdenas regime followed from the March 1938 nationalization of Mexico's oil fields. Although Mexicans largely supported the act, it incurred severe international sanctions along with internal challenges. In the months following the nationalization, Cárdenas made a series of broadcasts designed to calm the political seas, both nationally and internationally, and to answer the backlash of conservative opposition. His May 16 speech, for example, defended Mexico against direct charges of "dictatorship" and "communism" at the same time that it stressed Mexico's internal peace and social tranquillity. At one point, the president confidently declared that "conditions for maintaining peace have never been better. . . . In the countryside there are no partisans [*banderías*]; nor would the campesinos go against their own interests; their social demands have been satisfied" (Cárdenas, 1978:298). The speech specifically addressed the rebellious activities of General Saturnio Cedillo in San Luis Potosí. Having dismissed the possibility of rebellion in the countryside, Cárdenas particularly noted: "There is absolute tranquillity in this region; General Cedillo will not take up arms" (Cárdenas, 1978:300). Cárdenas presented a picture of a stable and orderly polity while glossing over ongoing hardship, privation, and opposition in the countryside.

Unfortunately for Cárdenas, General Cedillo *did* take up arms. Within weeks of the broadcast Cárdenas was forced to travel to San Luis Potosí, where he made no fewer than three major radio speeches and held a national press conference in response to the rebellion. His May 30 speech addressed both the Cedillo crisis and the oil crisis more broadly. On the occasion of the U.S. Day of the Unknown Soldier (Memorial Day), Cárdenas expressed his hope for better U.S.-Mexican relations and attempted to assure both his national and international audiences of Mexico's fundamental stability and commitment to the rule of law. He emphasized the importance of peace and democracy to Mexico, which, he said, "strives to turn the law into the guide of her conduct, equally in foreign as in domestic matters" (Cárdenas, 1978:304). Overall, the president used radio's ability to transcend the local context of action and make national claims about the Mexican polity to great advantage during these crisis periods.

Gritos Electrónicos

The first grito was sounded by Father Hidalgo in 1810 to rouse his parishioners to take up arms against the Spanish crown. The grito, originally a cry of "Death to the Spaniards [*Gachupines*]! Long live the Virgin of Guadalupe!" became part of the ritual celebration of Mexican independence (Krauze, 1997a:12). On the eve of Independence Day in Mexico City's Zocalo, the president still rings Hidalgo's bell and cries the grito ("¡Viva México! ¡Viva la Revolución!") in front of a crowd of thousands, who respond with their own cries of "¡Viva!" Under Mexico's activist, post-revolutionary state, radio offered a means of revolutionizing and nationalizing the grito. Beginning with the first government broadcasting stations in the 1920s, the grito was no longer confined to Independence Day, but—in its newly empowered electronic form—became a virtually constant flow of government propaganda. The PNR station, XEFO, in particular designed its gritos to activate and organize the "sons of the Revolution" through the institutional framework of the party. At the level of the presidency, however, the grito continued to take the form of a single, fatherly voice rallying popular support for a specific revolutionary cause.

An especially clear example of this kind of broadcast took place shortly after the election of President Cárdenas in July 1934. Former president Calles addressed a national audience to voice his support for the new president and to reassert his own position of power. Known as the "Grito de Guadalajara," the speech was broadcast from Guadalajara over station XED in network with Mexico City station XEB. In a brief and eloquent proclamation, Calles rallied his listeners to a new phase of the Revolution. "The eternal enemies watch [the Revolution] and attempt to negate its triumphs," he said. "It is necessary for us to begin a new period of Revolution, one that I will call psychological revolution; we must enter and take possession of the consciousness of the children, the consciousness of youth, because they do, and must, belong to the Revolution" (*Excelsior*, 1934a). Invoking the filial duty of Mexican youth toward the goals of the Revolution, Calles called for a reinvigorated anticlericalism focused on educational reform. Using the power of the radio grito, Calles voiced his political vision and pushed educational reform to the fore as a key policy issue for the Cárdenas administration.

President Cárdenas also used the radio on numerous occasions to announce new initiatives and rally popular support for them. Along with broadcasts on socialist education and the reorganization of the PNR, the president delivered the oil nationalization speech of March 18, 1938. Followed immediately by a full English-language translation, the speech addressed both national and international audiences. Cárdenas described the nationalization as an act of "economic emancipation" and provided a detailed account and justification of his decision. Following the tradition of the grito, the president called for the direct action and support of all Mexicans. He demanded absolute loyalty to his government and encouraged each citizen to act resourcefully and generously to combat the economic crisis that was sure to follow the nationalization. The speech was met with visible popular support in the form of thousands of public demonstrations across the country and thousands of telegrams sent directly to the president.

Cárdenas and the Radio Medium

Before examining the oil nationalization speech in more depth, it is necessary to explore the unique relationship between the Cárdenas regime and the radio medium. First, it is critical to point out that Cárdenas was well aware that radio could not reach the majority of Mexicans whom he considered his core constituency: the campesinos and laborers located in rural areas and working-class neighborhoods. Thus, his treks around the country (*gira*) were an essential and visible means of making contact with that constituency (Knight, 1998). He rode by train, car, and horse, and (famously) even swam to the farthest hamlets. During his presidential campaign, Cárdenas visited all twenty-eight states and territories, traveling over twenty-seven thousand kilometers of often difficult terrain (Weyl and Weyl, 1939). Yet the importance of the gira did not prevent Cárdenas from investing heavily in radio as a means of political communication; for example, by distributing hundreds of radios to his supporters in rural villages and working-class neighborhoods. His well-known "radio train"—which contained both sending and receiving equipment—also signaled his commitment to the new medium (Martin, 1935).

As with the gira, Cárdenas first turned to broadcasting during his presidential campaign. His campaign broadcasts were coordinated by Guillermo Morales Blumenkron, an experienced broadcaster who started his career at government station XERC in 1927, headed station XEFO at the age of twenty-six, and then became manager of DAPP station XEDP. Although Morales Blumenkron went on to become a successful commercial broadcaster, he continued to aid the official party in broadcasting matters and even served as coordinator for the radio campaign of President Gustavo Díaz Ordaz (1964–70) (Mejía Barquera, 1989; Miller, 1998). Morales Blumenkron appears to have been instrumental in encouraging Cárdenas to institutionalize broadcasting as part of his administration. A key element of the new president's radio policy was the tradition of New Year's broadcasts established on January 1, 1935. The first New Year's broadcast—made over a network of twenty-one of the country's most powerful stations—was also an early attempt to cover the entire national territory with a single transmission. According to Morales Blumenkron's exaggerated estimate, the broadcast reached four million people in Mexico and as many abroad (one to two million listeners in Mexico is a more realistic estimate) (Mejía Barquera, 1989).

The New Year's broadcasts combined two key functions. First, the speeches constituted an act of generosity, a gift, from the chief executive to the people. As such, each broadcast called for a reciprocal response on the part of the people in the form of solidarity and loyalty to the elected government. The New Year's address of 1938, for example, illustrates the typical message that concluded or initiated each broadcast: "On this New Year's Day I send my cordial greetings to the people of the Republic with my fervent desires that joy and prosperity will reach the very bosom of each and every home" (*Excelsior*, 1938:7). Second, each speech provided an accounting of the previous year's accomplishments and a statement of future goals. The bulk of the speech resembled a formal government report and typically lasted as long as one or two hours. Over the course of Cárdenas's six-year term, the occasion of the New Year's speech became increasingly ceremonial. For example, while the setting of the 1935 speech received little attention from the Mexico City press, in 1936 and 1937 the description of officials attending the ceremony became increasingly detailed. In 1936, *Excelsior* emphasized the gravity of the occasion by noting that the president's speech, delivered in a "slow and serene voice," was heard by the senators, cabinet members, and army officers present "with full attention and under the greatest silence" (*Excelsior*, 1936:1). To underline the importance of the event and ensure a broad audience, loudspeakers were set up in numerous public plazas around the city (*Excelsior*, 1937).

The regularization of presidential broadcasts was motivated, in part, by an interest in generating active public support for the regime. Cárdenas made every effort to ensure that his broadcasts reached as large an audience as possible. At the same time, he made sure that he heard the public's responses to his proclamations and policies. Not only did he receive public petitions as part of his daily routine, he also encouraged the public to contact him by means of the telegraph (Townsend, 1952; Becker, 1995). Immediately following his inauguration, Cárdenas declared that for one hour each day the telegraph would be free to any citizen desiring to communicate with the president. In this way, Cárdenas initiated a system of two-way communication between the president and the people—albeit a profoundly unequal one.

Despite his investment in the new medium, President Cárdenas was never described as a skilled radio speaker. Rather, he was characterized as a soft-spoken person for whom any speech "required a conscious effort" (Martin, 1935:3). An overview of the president's radio speeches, which he normally read directly from a prepared text, reveals a highly dense and bureaucratic style. Although one reporter detected a "new force" of self-righteousness in the president's speeches following the oil nationalization, even his admirers were apt to describe him as an uninspired speaker (Kluckhohn, 1938:3).[2] His radio style, in the words of one scholar, involved "very little oratory" (Townsend, 1952:176). Why, then, did Lázaro Cárdenas make radio such a central part of his administration?

Cárdenas understood that radio was especially well suited to Mexican politics because of its ability to reach and unite Mexico's far-flung citizens. Indeed, as Cárdenas himself noted, the Mexican "people are profoundly auditory and radio can be a factor of inestimable effectiveness for the integration of a national mentality" (Mejía Barquera, 1989:63, n. 4). At the same time that Cárdenas described the auditory capacity of Mexicans as a kind of physical condition, he also described radio as a material force that could bind individuals together through a shared mentality. Cárdenas further developed the notion of a material or tactile connection between the radio speaker and radio listener when, in one campaign speech, he stated: "I want to make my voice reach out to each and every worker in the Republic" (*Excelsior*, 1934b). Commentator Félix Palavicini expressed a similar view of the physicality of radio when he observed that, through radio, "the leader of the country, reaches even to the heart of his fellow citizens and not in the cold form of print, but in the communicative warmth of the spoken word" (Leyva, 1992:66). From this perspective, radio extended the "warmth" of bodily contact through the emotional force of the spoken word. Not only could the president's voice touch each listener, but this touch could connect the listeners to each other and materialize the body politic through the medium of radio.

Call and Response

Although the oil nationalization was an extraordinary event in Mexican history, the radio speech announcing it was in many ways an ordinary presidential broadcast. The speech was long and dense and provided complex legal and historical justifications for the expropriation. Cárdenas included poignant examples of the foreign oil corporations' disparaging treatment of Mexican workers and their disdain for Mexican sovereignty. At three different points in the speech the president called on his listeners to provide the "moral and material support" necessary to back the government's "revolutionary" action. In his final repetition of the call, the president exclaimed: "From the people I ask only full confidence and absolute support [*respaldo absoluto*] for the measures that their own government was forced to make" (Cárdenas, 1978:287).

As this excerpt indicates, the speech hailed listeners on a number of levels. First, the president spoke in his own voice to ask for the listeners' personal loyalty to him and direct reciprocation of his declaration. For example, when he said that "I ask only full confidence and absolute support," he spoke as an individual who was also the president of Mexico. In his role as president, Cárdenas spoke on behalf of the central state and its institutions. Listeners were asked to support "the government" in the measures it had taken. But as nationalism scholars have noted, the state's active role in civil society is almost always justified as an expression of "the national interest" (Poulantzas, 1978; Blanco 1982). Thus, the primary level at which listeners were called on was in their roles as members of the Mexican nation. Indeed, Cárdenas used the term "nation" a dozen times in his address and made numerous references to "Mexico," "the republic," "our country," "our laws," and "our progress." National allegiance was thus the focus of the address despite the fact that the rights of Mexican labor, and the government's support of them, was at the core of the petroleum controversy. Cárdenas did not address "the workers" or "our laboring classes" on this occasion, but spoke to "all of the sectors of the nation" (Cárdenas, 1978:287).

While public reaction to the oil expropriation has been widely reported in terms of the public demonstrations and mass donations of personal wealth made in the wake of the decree (Ruíz, 1992; Krauze, 1997b), the telegrams sent to the president in direct response to the speech have been largely ignored. These telegrams, which document the immediate reactions of individuals and groups from a wide range of social sectors, were sent directly to the president through the channel of communication that he had singled out and institutionalized for such use. A total of 392 telegrams were examined from a collection held as part of the Petroleum Conflict records in the Lázaro Cárdenas presidential branch of the National Archives in Mexico City (Cárdenas, 1938). All 392 telegrams came from a single folder of congratulations sent on March 18 and 19.[3] An analysis of these telegrams reveals the dialogic quality of the public's response to the president's call and sheds new light on the role of broadcasting in articulating the paternal authority of the president.

The telegrams came from a wide range of individuals and groups from every state and territory in the country. The Town Council of Metepex, Oaxaca, sent a telegram (via Toluca, Mexico), as did the Oil Workers' Union of Macuspana, Tabasco; the governor of Zacatecas; the ejidatarios of Tixkokob, Yucatán (via Motul, Yucatán); and the Union of Veterinary Doctors in Mexico City. The majority of telegrams came from the central states and Mexico City, while a smaller percentage came from the northern and southern states and territories.

Following the abbreviated, condensed, and often ungrammatical form of the medium, the telegrams range in length from a few sentences to several paragraphs. A short telegram from Mazatlan, Sinaloa, simply states: "SECTION 36 DOCK WORKERS UNION MEXICAN REPUBLIC SUPPORT ABSOLUTELY YOUR GOVERNMENT OIL MATTER. SEC. GEN. JOSE M. HERNANDEZ" (Cárdenas, 1938:no. 51). A more typical telegram from Monterrey, Nuevo Leon, goes into greater detail: "EXECUTIVE COMMITTEE SECTION 19 RAILROAD UNION, IN THE NAME OF ALL MEMBERS REGISTER OUR COMPLETE AD-HERENCE AND ABSOLUTE SUPPORT [*RESPALDO ABSOLUTO*] FOR VIRILE ATTITUDE TAKEN ON OIL CONFLICT, READY FOR ANY SACRIFICE IN ORDER TO RESPOND AND HELP YOU TAKE MEASURES TO SAVE OUR BELOVED COUNTRY, WAITING TO

FOLLOW INSTRUCTIONS TO ACHIEVE THE SALVATION OF OUR HONORED COUNTRY. PLEASE RECEIVE OUR MOST SINCERE CONGRATULATIONS ON YOUR DIGNIFIED ATTITUDE. WE SALUTE YOU. BY EXECUTIVE COMMITTEE. LOCAL SECRETARY OF ARRANGEMENTS. LOCAL SECRETARY. GUSTAVO GUTIERREZ. NICOLAS SALDANA" (Cárdenas, 1938:no. 12). Overall, the telegrams came from six broad categories of senders: labor unions (33 percent); ejidos and campesino groups (30 percent); private sector groups and individuals (15 percent); political groups and political officials (10 percent); teacher and professional unions (9 percent); and school and student groups (3 percent).

Almost one-third of the telegrams present their responses as direct reactions to the president's broadcast. Although only 5 percent specifically mention radio, almost a third make direct reference to the speech and mention, for example, "the sensational declarations made by you personally last night over the radio," "the message to the nation read by you last night," and "the patriotic speech delivered [*pronunciado*] last night" (Cárdenas, 1938:nos. 312, 33, 202). Factors that may have discouraged direct references to the broadcast in the majority of telegrams include the economy of expression required by telegraphy and the perceived "transparency" of the speech with the event of nationalization. That is, the facts that the speech was itself the act of nationalizing the oil fields and that radio provided a simultaneous and instantaneous experience of the event obscured the form in which it was communicated.

Nonetheless, most of the telegrams create a dialogue with the president's radio speech. First, all of the telegrams congratulate the president and provide some kind of affirmation or support for his action. A third of the telegrams directly reciprocate the president's call for "absolute support" by repeating his exact language (see the above examples). For example, one telegram from a workers' union in the Department of the Federal District in Mexico City proclaims "absolute support to the point of arms if necessary"; others offer to make "any sacrifice," including their own "blood" (Cárdenas, 1938:no. 287). Second, the telegrams offer support in the same terms that Cárdenas requested it: primarily as a matter of national allegiance. Almost half of the telegrams use the terms *nation, patria*, and *patriotic* to describe the president's action and to orient their own support of it.

For example, one telegram observes, "now that you have taught the country how to be free, we feel more Mexican than ever"; another sender claims to have discovered "the pride of being Mexican" through the president's declaration (Cárdenas, 1938:nos. 118, 364). Of the remaining telegrams, 10 percent combine class and national loyalties, 11 percent describe the government as the site of allegiance, and 35 percent identify only the president as the focus of loyalty and support.

The president is identified as the primary agent of political authority in almost all of the telegrams. Even in cases in which nation, class, or the state is the focus of allegiance, this allegiance is channeled through the president with such expressions as "your government," "your patriotic attitude," and "your working-class politics." The president's speech—"personally delivered"—provided a means through which a variety of allegiances could be invoked. In the telegram responses, Cárdenas is the individual authority to whom loyalty (often unconditional) is expressed. This authority takes on an overtly paternalist cast in the 14 percent of telegrams that specifically praise the president for his "virile" (*viril*), "brave" (*gallarda*), and "valiant" (*valiente*) action against the oil companies.

Although a handful of telegrams appear to be formulaic responses prompted by labor and political organizations (these telegrams use the exact same phrasing), it is difficult to interpret the telegram responses as simply another example of Mexico's officially orchestrated mass politics. The different layers of allegiance expressed and the importance of the president himself as a virile, paternal authority figure suggest a diversity of political experiences across the range of telegram writers. While a focus on the personal action and authority of the president may indicate traditional cacique politics, other expressions indicate a commitment to the new, nationalized political and labor organizations established during the Calles and Cárdenas regimes (Rubin, 1996; Knight, 1998). Evidently, however, the language of nation and patria—materialized through the voice of the president—was a central, organizing force in both the president's speech and in the majority of telegram responses. In sum, both the call and the response of the oil nationalization speech suggest that the paternal voice of the president provided an ideal medium through which the antimodern trajectories of radio and nation could be realized.

Presidential Broadcasting under Ávila Camacho and Alemán

After the oil nationalization and the economic crisis that followed, the government's project of progressivism waned and Cárdenas searched for a moderate successor to maintain and protect the reforms already in place. As Albert Michaels puts it, "Cárdenas's reforms had provoked hatred and anxiety among small landholders and the growing urban middle classes. A new president would be required to pacify these factors as well as worried foreign investors or the economy might completely collapse" (Michaels, 1970:52). While Manuel Ávila Camacho (1940–46) was a close protégé of Cárdenas, he was also a moderate politician who intended to rebuild the government's relationship with the right, particularly the Catholic Church. Well before the election, it was widely reported that he would encourage private capital and foreign investment and retreat from his mentor's progressive social agenda (*New York Times*, 1940).

In the area of broadcasting, however, Ávila Camacho continued Cárdenas's activist tradition. In part, his close ties to Cárdenas inspired continuity with the former president's radio strategies. In addition, Ávila Camacho had close connections of his own with broadcasting through his brother, Maximino, who became secretary of communications and transport, and his campaign adviser, Alonso Sordo Noriega, who was an experienced announcer and aspiring media mogul. Most important, though, the president found radio to be an indispensable—indeed, unavoidable—means of mass communication during World War II. The U.S. government in particular encouraged Ávila Camacho's use of the medium as part of its "Pan-American" propaganda campaign. Along with his first New Year's address, U.S. networks broadcast several of the president's key speeches to the North American public, including Mexico's declaration of war against the Axis (Ávila Camacho, 1940).

The New Year's broadcasts were an important point of continuity between Ávila Camacho and Cárdenas. His first broadcast of December 31, 1940, closely followed his predecessor's tradition and was given with ceremony from the national palace and broadcast to an international audience. Future speeches, however, were delivered with less fanfare from the presidential office and residence at Los Pinos. The New Year's speeches followed

Cárdenas's format: the president provided a progress report and called for the Mexican people's unity and commitment to his agenda. On December 31, 1944, for example, President Ávila Camacho offered a greeting of "encouragement and esteem" for all Mexicans and specifically called on all listeners to contribute morally and materially to the welfare of the nation (*Excelsior*, 1944). The following year, Ávila Camacho addressed his "compatriots" with "a message of affection and inalterable confidence in the destiny of the nation" (*Excelsior*, 1945). Like Cárdenas, Ávila Camacho used these national broadcasts to rouse the Mexican people—his "fellow citizens" (*conciudadanos*)—to a destiny that he described as a noble, national one.

The transition from Ávila Camacho to Miguel Alemán (1946–52), however, witnessed significant changes in presidential broadcasting. In contrast to Ávila Camacho, Alemán represented a final break with the Cárdenas era. The *New York Times* noted Alemán's further shift to the right and praised him as a "self made man" who would manage Mexico as a "business enterprise" (*New York Times*, 1946; Brenner, 1948). The discontinuity with the progressive tradition was clearly signaled by the absence of Cárdenas from Alemán's inauguration ceremony (Bracker, 1946). Unlike Ávila Camacho, Alemán represented a "new" Mexico. His key constituencies were not peasants and laborers but the growing urban middle class that desired U.S.-led development and consumer capitalism along with a strong dose of Christian tradition and patriarchal authority (Pérez Montfort, 1994; Acevedo-Muñoz, 1998).

Despite his break from Cárdenas, Alemán initially continued the activist approach to broadcasting. He delivered a New Year's address on January 1, 1947, and made numerous international broadcasts during a nine-day tour of the United States in May 1947. His New Year's address proclaimed a strong and clear statement of the new Mexico he envisioned: "The Mexican home is the nation [*patria*] itself—not in its political meaning—but in its moral significance" (*El Universal*, 1947). This focus on the Mexican (read middle-class) home and family as a model for national morality indicated the administration's vision of a privatized polity guided by social conservatism and personal accumulation.

After his initial New Year's broadcast, however, Alemán abruptly abandoned the tradition. In place of coverage of the New Year's address, Mexico

City papers provided brief notes that the president was vacationing in Cuernavaca and Acapulco (1948), Vera Cruz (1950), and again in Acapulco (1951).[4] On New Year's Eve 1949, perhaps in response to a growing sense of economic crisis (in June the peso was devalued for the second time in a year), the president resumed the New Year's broadcast. Alemán did not deliver the speech, however; instead, Secretary of the Interior Adolfo Ruíz Cortines spoke in the president's place, to wish "happiness [*ventura*] to the people and homes of the nation" and request the faith, hard work, and confidence of the people (*El Universal*, 1950). Ruíz Cortines did not speak as secretary of the interior; he delivered the speech as written for the president. The headline published in *El Universal*—"The President Asks for Trust in Work and Confidence in Mexico"—gave no indication of the switch in speakers. In part, the replacement of the president was an opportunity for the secretary to try his presidential wings before being named as official successor the following year. However, it also indicated the emptiness of the presidential broadcast: the president's speech could easily be ventriloquized in his absence.

This notion of ventriloquism is particularly apt in describing the Alemán regime and its relationship to Mexican political culture. Enrique Krauze illustrates this in his discussion of Rudolfo Usigli's play *The Impostor* (*El gesticulador*). The play, originally written in the late 1930s, opened at Bellas Artes in May 1947 and was abruptly canceled on government orders.[5] *The Imposter* tells the story of an official who takes credit for a revolutionary victory in which he never participated. According to Krauze, the play not only proclaims the death of the Revolution, but critiques the "lie of its perennial, institutional existence" (Krauze, 1997c:526). The impostor is not unlike a ventriloquist's dummy. When the ventriloquist is discovered, however, he also turns out to be a dummy through which another impostor was speaking. The metaphor seems to fit Alemán's radio address: the voice behind the microphone could no longer be located in the labyrinth of government power and bureaucracy.

The transformation of presidential broadcasting from the style of Cárdenas to that of Alemán highlights the crisis of official ideology in the postwar era. Cárdenas used radio to extend the grain, or the body, of the president's voice to his listening audience (Barthes, 1990). Through that voice the president aimed to evoke allegiance not only to his own, paternal authority, but to the nation as a community of sentiment and commitment. Telegrams sent in reaction to the speech suggest that listeners were moved by the president's "personal" radio appeal to express their allegiance and commitment to both Cárdenas and the nation represented by, and through, his speech. Alemán, however, following his own vision of private initiative and personal accumulation, was hardly in a position to encourage public commitment. The voice of the president, as articulated through the radio medium, became a mere ventriloquism of a government authority and ideology that seemed, itself, to be empty of meaning.

Radio at War

(Pan-)Americanism on the Air

This chapter returns to the subject that introduced this book: Mexican broadcasting during World War II. While Chapter 1 used this example to outline the social relations that shaped both the development of radio broadcasting and nation formation in Mexico, the present chapter examines wartime broadcasting in more depth in order to clarify how two key actors—the U.S. Coordinator of Inter-American Affairs (CIAA) and the Azcárraga Group—negotiated the structure and content of Mexican radio during the war years.

U.S. Broadcasters and the Good Neighbor Policy

As discussed in Chapter 3, important barriers separated North American broadcasters from Latin American listeners during the 1930s, including technological limitations, cultural differences, and relatively weak broadcasting markets. The main presence of North American broadcasters in Latin America was via shortwave radio from transmitters located in the United States. In the mid-1930s, six corporations had shortwave operations aimed at Latin America: CBS, NBC, General Electric, Westinghouse, Crosley, and a nonprofit broadcaster, the World Wide Broadcasting Corporation. Of these companies, the majority were involved in shortwave broadcasting to promote the sale of their electrical equipment in the region—including NBC, which promoted RCA products.[1]

Although both NBC and CBS began shortwave broadcasting as early as 1930, their initial interest in the medium was to bring foreign programs to listeners in the United States rather than to develop a full-scale shortwave broadcasting venture. Indeed, the U.S. Federal Radio Commission had classified shortwave as an experimental service that could not be operated for profit. In addition, shortwave was subject to a great deal of atmospheric interference and was of much poorer quality than local AM radio transmissions. By the mid-1930s the United States was still receiving three times as many international shortwave broadcasts as it was making (Fejes, 1986). All of this began to change in 1936, when an improvement in shortwave technology and a new interest on the part of the Roosevelt administration in the security of Latin American markets combined to make North American broadcasters much more interested in sending shortwave transmissions to Latin America.

The Roosevelt administration's focus on interhemispheric cooperation —the Good Neighbor Policy—was a diplomatic initiative to open Latin American markets to North American goods and build hemispheric solidarity on the basis of increased commercial and cultural exchange and communication. It was also a specific effort to counteract Germany's growing economic and political activities in Latin America, which were fundamentally associated in the minds of Washington policy makers with the threat of local anti-American, or "fifth column," movements (Haglund, 1984). Much of the concern about fifth column activities was generated by the onslaught of Axis propaganda broadcasts in the region. By the end of the decade, German and Italian shortwave broadcasts were much more powerful and reportedly more influential than transmissions from the United States (Fejes, 1986).

In response to this perceived threat, between 1937 and 1938 two major proposals were brought before the U.S. Congress to create government-owned shortwave stations to counteract the German propaganda broadcasts (Fejes, 1986). NBC and CBS reacted to these proposals (which were never enacted) by greatly increasing their investment in shortwave in order to prove to the Roosevelt administration that commercial broadcasters were fully capable of representing U.S. strategic interests in Latin America. Primarily, the networks were motivated by their fear that the New Deal administration would use international broadcasting as an "entering wedge" to develop government broadcasting on the domestic front (Deihl, 1977; Fejes, 1986; McChesney, 1990).

The imperative of serving U.S. government interests in Latin America shaped not only the networks' investments in shortwave technology but also the content and goals of network shortwave broadcasts. In 1938, for example, NBC network administrators discussed the need to maintain close contact with "those Washington government circles which are interested in South American relations and South American trade" (Mason, 1938:3).[2] Not surprisingly, the network executives believed that news programming would be one of the best ways to fulfill government expectations in Latin America. A 1941 CBS press release described this objective in the following terms: "The programs will be designed to promote better relations with the United States and are 'built' here specifically to interest listeners in the southern republics . . . and to supply them with the complete news—unbiased and uncolored—in the American way" (CBS, 1941:2). NBC internal memos and reports, however, reveal the networks' more strategic aim of using news broadcasts to represent U.S. government policy; for example: "News is the backbone of the service of the International Division. . . . Naturally an effort should be made to put our right foot forward. No propaganda. . . . Equally naturally, we accept as axiomatic the validity of the foreign policy of the government. We present that policy as is. We mention in succinct summarization those criticisms of it which are truly pertinent. Thus we tell the whole story but in terms of the relative values which must exist outside rather than inside our frontier" (Winner, 1938:1). The report went on to predict that "we should gradually be able to become the authentic radio instrumentality of the foreign policies of the government" (Winner, 1938:2). Clearly, NBC executives recognized the interlocking interests of the government and the network: the network would act as a direct representative of U.S. foreign policy so that the government would stay out of the radio business.

Although the FCC reclassified shortwave from an experimental service to a commercial broadcasting service in late 1939, direct shortwave broadcasting seemed unlikely to become a profitable venture because very few Latin Americans had radios capable of receiving shortwave signals (the Southern Cone, with significant numbers of "all-wave" radios and committed shortwave listeners, was an exception). Shortwave broadcasts could be retransmitted over local Latin American stations for better audience coverage, but this practice was relatively rare because shortwave signals were of poor quality. Despite financial losses, however, the networks continued their limited broadcasting programs as a show of "national" strength against the powerful broadcasts of the German and Italian governments.

Even after CBS and NBC signed affiliation agreements with Latin American stations in 1940 and 1941, the networks' investments in the region remained limited. NBC's 1941 affiliation agreements with 117 stations were for a period of one year and did not require affiliates to broadcast a minimum amount of NBC programming (as was required of North American affiliates) (NBC, 1941). Indeed, NBC International Division chief John Royal stated that he never expected Latin American stations to carry NBC rebroadcasts on a regular basis for the same reason that U.S. networks rarely carried shortwave programs: their quality was unpredictable, they were difficult to schedule, and they were expensive. Royal did, however, expect Latin American stations to rebroadcast a few special programs sent by shortwave from the United States, including "the Toscanini concerts, the Metropolitan Opera, the prize fights, and other important American programs" (Royal, 1941:6). Although CBS had hopes of building a profitable Latin American network at some future time, its relations with Latin American stations were also quite informal. The 1940 CBS contracts with 64 Latin American radio stations covered a five-year period and required the stations to broadcast just one hour per day of CBS programming (Fejes, 1986). Shortwave offered NBC and CBS a simple and effective means of establishing informal relations with Latin American stations without having to invest in AM radio technology or make major economic commitments to Latin American affiliates.

Although North American networks tried to make a good showing in Latin America, their small-scale ventures could not compete with the well-financed German and Italian shortwave campaigns. As one contemporary observed: "Our programs to Latin America were beamed to the big cities, which were the big markets for our goods. U.S. broadcasters engaged in the job not so much for profit as for the prestige, publicity, research, and to help the Government—or, say skeptics, to keep Uncle Sam out of radio broadcasting. The job was big and costly. Some networks were spending up to $200,000 a year. Advertising couldn't meet the bill (Josephs, 1945b:26).

Eventually, President Roosevelt appointed Nelson Rockefeller to direct the CIAA with the mission of expanding and subsidizing private U.S. broadcasting (and other media) enterprises in Latin America. Established by executive order in August 1940, the CIAA marked a new kind of cultural diplomacy aimed at the mass publics of other countries rather than just foreign governments or diplomats (Fejes, 1986). As a flexible and economical means of reaching mass audiences, radio broadcasting became an integral part of this new diplomatic strategy.

The Government-Business Partnership

The fact that the CIAA was a partnership of U.S. government and private business interests shaped both the administrative structure and the propaganda objectives of the agency. Most obvious, perhaps, was the appointment of Rockefeller, a private citizen with enormous business interests in Latin America via Standard Oil and Chase Manhattan Bank and through his close connections with RCA in New York, as director. While some viewed Rockefeller's economic ties as a conflict of interest, by the logic of the cooperative state—in which the government used its organizations and resources to support commercial expansion—these associations could only enhance the state's ability to coordinate and promote U.S. business and industry abroad (Hawley, 1974; Deihl, 1977; Rosenberg, 1982).

Despite numerous government efforts to consolidate wartime propaganda activities, Rockefeller maintained his agency's autonomy from the Office of War Information (OWI) (CIAA, 1947). Specifically, Rockefeller fought to protect a cooperative government-industry approach to Latin American relations that he believed would both combat the Axis influence and lay the foundation for enhanced economic opportunities in the postwar era. While the OWI aimed to win the war by "undermining [U.S.] enemies and encouraging [and] directing the resistance of the peoples of the conquered countries," Rockefeller was "building for permanent, successful, fruitful, inter-American relationships in the post-war period" (CIAA, 1943c:1–2).

The CIAA's budget grew from an initial $3.5 million in 1941 to a wartime high of more than $60 million, with a large percentage of that going to support the agency's information activities. The Information Division comprised the Radio, Film, and Press Divisions, all of which were operated by "dollar-a-year" volunteer executives from major U.S. advertising and media firms. As noted in Chapter 1, the Radio Division chief was Donald Francisco, vice president of the Lord and Thomas advertising agency. The Radio Division operated with a staff of only 125 (compared with 647 people employed in similar activities by the OWI) because the majority of the production activities remained in the hands of private broadcasters. Under CIAA directives, these private broadcasting companies produced radio programs that were distributed throughout Latin America via shortwave radio and recorded programs and scripts (CIAA, 1947).

Along with administrators located in Washington, D.C., and New York City, the CIAA was aided by field agents and coordination committees of U.S. citizens located in individual Latin American countries. The Coordination Committee for Mexico was chaired by James R. Woodul, general manager of the American Smelting Company. The Communications subcommittee included corporate executives from North American electronics and advertising firms and general managers of companies that advertised heavily in the Mexican market (Coca-Cola, Colgate Palmolive, and Sydney Ross–Sterling Drugs) (CIAA, 1943a). Radio operations were under the direction of field agent and public relations expert Herbert Cerwin, a fluent Spanish speaker who worked with a staff that eventually included about two hundred Mexican nationals (Cerwin, 1966). Cerwin and the CIAA subcommittee worked closely with Mexican broadcasters and Mexican-based U.S. advertisers to produce programs for distribution throughout the Mexican radio market.

While the CIAA coordinated private activities and directly sponsored press, radio, and film campaigns in the region, one of its most significant actions was gaining U.S. Treasury Department subsidies for corporate advertising in Latin America. Under Rockefeller's powerful persuasion, the Treasury Department issued a ruling in early 1942 that "for the first time in U.S. history, allow[ed] manufacturers to deduct from their corporation income tax, a 'reasonable amount' for advertising and promotional activities in foreign markets" (CIAA, 1942c:3). Rockefeller was also personally responsible for urging hundreds of companies to maintain or increase their levels of advertising in Latin America as a contribution to the war effort (Fejes, 1986; Ortiz Garza, 1989). Advertisers were asked to include CIAA slogans or other forms of pro-U.S. propaganda in their advertising campaigns.

Another major CIAA activity was the elimination of what the agency perceived as "anti-American" individuals (defined as anyone who was not vocally pro-American) working in Latin American businesses, especially media organizations. This was accomplished through an all-out campaign of blacklisting and advertiser boycotts which had succeeded in quieting most of the prominent pro-Axis voices in Mexico and most Latin American countries by mid-1942 (Green, 1971). Blanca Torres Ramírez reports that the CIAA campaign was one of the key factors in transforming the editorial stance of Mexico City newspapers from a neutral or pro-Axis view to a pro-U.S. perspective in just a matter of months (Torres Ramírez, 1979).[3] Similarly, the Rockefeller Committee took vigorous steps to identify and eliminate Mexican radio broadcasters whom it believed to be anti-American (CIAA, 1947).

The CIAA-Network Partnership

The agency's first act was to encourage private broadcasters to increase the power of their shortwave transmitters and improve the accessibility of their programs to Latin American listeners. In 1941 Francisco met with the private broadcasting companies and "informed them that it would be necessary to improve reception of programs in the other American republics before substantial aid could be advanced by CIAA" (CIAA, 1946b:5). Such "aid" consisted of sponsorship for programs produced by the six shortwave broadcasters and the creation of a central office for editing and translating news items for broadcast to Latin America. Programs to be sponsored included musical programs, rebroadcasts of North American network programs, and special broadcasts of presidential addresses (CIAA, 1946b:9).

After the United States entered the war, the CIAA took an increasingly active role in shortwave broadcasting and reorganized broadcasting resources in order to increase the number of transmitters from fourteen to thirty-six. Effective November 1, 1942, the CIAA leased time on all privately owned shortwave stations. According to the contracts the CIAA signed with the shortwave broadcasters, "two-thirds of the time leased was allotted by agreement to OWI and one-third to CIAA, and payment for facilities were in the same proportion" (CIAA, 1946b:13). These contracts were renewed every year until June 20, 1946. Under these leasing agreements, NBC and CBS continued to do the majority of CIAA programming—that is, "while CBS and NBC under the contract did the writing of scripts, final authority for all programming rested with the CIAA" (CIAA, 1946a:16).

Along with news programs the networks produced dramatizations of war-related news such as *We Are at War* (*Estamos en guerra*), *Ideas Cannot Be Killed* (*Las ideas no se matan*), and *The March of Time* (*La marcha del tiempo*), which summarized weekly news development and emphasized the physical and moral strength of the Allied nations. Programs such as *Counterespionage* (*Contraespionaje*), *The Mysterious One* (*El misterioso*), and *The Spirit of Victory* (*Espíritu de victoria*) presented serialized stories of pro-Allies heroes and anti-Axis wartime adventures and intrigues. In addition to these programs there were musical broadcasts, including *El hit parade*, which featured North American popular music. As will be discussed further below, these programs were augmented by programs produced in Mexico by the Mexican Coordination Committee of the CIAA.

As the war went on, CIAA officials felt the need to improve shortwave coverage; on July 1, 1943, they relocated shortwave transmitters and combined the NBC and CBS programs into a single Spanish-language service (CIAA, 1946b:15). After this date, NBC and CBS programs were transmitted during alternative hours on a single frequency. In 1945 the government took over the shortwave stations, but the networks continued providing programs until 1948, when the service was transferred to the State Department and designated the Voice of America. During the war years, and perhaps even more so in the cold war era, it became clear to both the U.S. government and private broadcasters that commercial broadcasting alone could not meet the state's strategic broadcasting needs in developing and Communist-bloc countries. Commercial broadcasters acquiesced, in part because they no longer viewed government broadcasting in the international arena as a threat to commercial broadcasting in the domestic sphere. In addition, U.S. networks became increasingly distracted from international radio by their investments in the new medium of television (Fejes, 1986).

"To Sell the Listener on the U.S.": CIAA Propaganda Objectives

Although CIAA broadcasts relentlessly chanted the mantras "Pan-Americanism" and "Americas United" (*Américas unidas*), the agency's main objective was to create pro-U.S. sentiments in Latin America by exporting a subtle version of nationalist discourse. This discourse can be traced through the propaganda directives issued to guide network program production. In December 1941, for example, the CIAA described the goal of its shortwave broadcasts as "sound radio showmanship" designed to "create a flow of outstanding program attractions which would reveal the American nation as a powerful, personable, friendly, idealistic neighbor who is at war, and who will win its war" (Fejes, 1986:144, n. 65). By April 1942, the agency defined its main objective as "the development of a deep respect for this country and its inevitable victory in the present war" and the creation of "the conviction on the part of Latin America that cooperation with the United States is essentially practical now and in the future" (Robbins, 1942). These goals were essential to the CIAA's long-range plan to build "good will and consumer acceptance for U.S. products as groundwork to our post-war trade" (CIAA, 1942c:2).

As the direction of the war changed in early 1943 and the Allies no longer viewed Hitler as a military threat to Latin America, CIAA administrators changed their propaganda objectives accordingly. Now that it appeared that the Allies would win and the United States would become a dominant global power, the CIAA aimed to decrease the emphasis on U.S. power and resources and deemphasize "any appearance of United States imperialism in Latin America." The CIAA directive continued: "Likewise in the cultural field, we should be careful not to emphasize moves which would indicate that we were imposing our cultural ideas, publications, or other media of expression upon those countries because of our superior technical and economic resources" (CIAA, 1943b:2). Nonetheless, the objective of creating a positive image of the United States remained the agency's first priority. For example, an April 1943 directive stated that 75 percent of CIAA information activities aimed to create a positive image of the United States, whereas only 25 percent aimed to relate the progress of the war. The directive emphasized that the goal of every CIAA radio program was to "sell the listener on the U.S."—equating government propaganda with an advertiser's sales pitch (CIAA, 1943c:1–2).

In late 1943 and 1944, CIAA propaganda shifted again to meet the hemisphere's changing situation. The new problem on the horizon was how to deal with growing Latin American discontent over wartime shortages, although the question of U.S. domination in the postwar period continued to be a concern. Programs for Mexican audiences were directed to "stress our policy in liberated countries to show we have no imperialistic aims" and emphasize that "Mexico and the U.S. have much to give each other from their individual cultures without weakening either" (CIAA, 1944). In response to the problem of wartime shortages and economic dislocations —which brought starvation to the Mexican countryside—CIAA officials stressed the interdependence of the U.S. and Mexican economies (Torres Ramírez, 1979; Niblo, 1988). "A raised standard of living in Mexico and Latin America is equally beneficial to the U.S., Mexico, and all Latin America," stated one directive (CIAA, 1944). Through a range of news, commentary, music, and dramatic programs the CIAA constructed a discourse of "Americanism" for Latin American consumption. In part, this was an effort to "internationalize" the state-sponsored nationalism that the U.S. government had been developing domestically over the course of the 1930s through government radio projects and other prominent cultural activities (Sayre, 1941; Alexander, 1980; Hayes, 1994). State-sponsored nationalism represented a newly legitimated expression of state power that CIAA officials believed would work just as successfully in the international arena as it had within the boundaries of the United States. In a world of increasingly international, mass-mediated politics, U.S. officials looked to an expansive discourse of "American" nationalism to provide a narrative of national development and achievement capable of incorporating Latin American client states into a hemispheric union.

The CIAA's Ideal versus Azcárraga's Reality

In Mexico, and throughout Latin America, CIAA operatives encountered a broadcasting reality quite different from the situation they had envisioned when planning their propaganda initiatives. This divergence between ideal and reality appeared at two general levels: the format or delivery of radio programs and the content of radio programs. An analysis of these areas of divergence reveals the process of negotiation between the CIAA and the Azcárraga organization that shaped both the form and content of Mexican broadcasting.

Program Delivery

It became evident early on that CIAA administrators held an unrealistic view of the ability of shortwave broadcasting to reach the Latin American public. While they focused on increasing the power of shortwave transmitters, CIAA officials were slow to discover what both North American networks and Axis broadcasters already knew: most Latin Americans did not listen to international shortwave radio. As Cerwin succinctly observed in 1942: "Short wave appears to be a flop; unlike South America there are only a limited number of short-wave sets in Mexico. Furthermore, because of the surrounding mountains, the reception is usually bad and cannot be counted upon" (Cerwin, 1942:2). To reach a mass audience it was necessary to broadcast programs over local AM stations. CIAA organizers planned to solve this problem by having local stations retransmit shortwave broadcasts, but this approach also proved inappropriate to the local reality. Many Mexican stations lacked the technology to receive and retransmit shortwave signals without considerable interference. For example, Mexico's most powerful station, XEW, had only one shortwave receiver located in its downtown studio, which was insufficient to ensure high-quality retransmission. To improve the broadcast quality Azcárraga would have had to install at least two expensive directional antennae outside the city limits—a purchase he was unable or unwilling to make (Williams, 1942). Azcárraga told NBC's John Royal that if NBC wanted his affiliate stations to rebroadcast these programs, it would have to pay higher rates to cover the added expenses (Azcárraga, 1942).

The best solution to the problem proved to be the use of high-quality recordings (electrical transcriptions) to distribute radio programs to Latin American stations. Initially the CIAA had intended to use electrical transcriptions only as a means of reaching small radio stations that produced few live programs and lacked the equipment to rebroadcast shortwave transmissions (CIAA, 1942b:28). However, officials soon discovered that Latin America's most powerful and popular stations preferred to use recordings; not only did they offer the fidelity that shortwave rebroadcasts lacked, but they were also more easily incorporated into the busy schedules of these large commercial stations (Azcárraga, 1942). As XEW assistant manager José Milmo explained to Royal after the station failed to retransmit an important shortwave broadcast, scheduling was a significant problem: "All of our evening time is commercially sponsored and most accounts occupying evening time have their exclusive singers, directors and talent of their programas [sic] upon monthly salaries. Never the less we are willing and will retransmit all important events that will aid towards hemisphere solidarity but we must have advance information upon same" (Milmo, 1942). Although the Azcárraga organization agreed to rebroadcast special-event programs such as speeches by President Roosevelt, at times it was not able to carry even these programs because of prior commitments.

Indeed, the use of recordings gave Azcárraga considerable control over the timing of CIAA broadcasts; he could plug them into the existing XEW schedule wherever it was convenient. The recordings could also be shipped to XEW affiliate stations across the country for broadcast to local audiences (Francisco, 1942). Such recordings, however, bypassed the use of XEW's staff and facilities and thus did not generate the same level of revenue as locally produced programs. In response, Azcárraga instituted a 50 percent surcharge for time on XEW that was filled with electrical transcription programs.

Another solution that fit the Mexican reality was the local production of radio programs by the CIAA's Coordination Committee for Mexico. Such programs had the benefit of meshing with the tone and style of Mexican radio. Shortwave programs sounded foreign to Mexican listeners, who preferred programs oriented to their domestic interests and concerns. As Francisco explained, "none of our shortwave commentators are rebroadcast in Mexico . . . because the [CIAA Mexico] Committee has two commentators with a Mexican accent who interpret the news from the viewpoint of the Mexican audience" (Francisco, 1943:3). In addition to news programs, the committee sponsored a series of short public-information programs that were broadcast daily over XEW. Cerwin's description of these programs is informative: "There is the morning program at 9:30 at which Señorita Dorantes speaks to the Mexican women; this is for ten minutes.

I have heard it several mornings and found it good, and the propaganda was handled in a subtle manner. From 1:15 to 1:25, there is news of the world, also slanted to our side; and at 9:10, there is a ten-minute news commentary" (Cerwin, 1942:3). The programs produced by the Coordination Committee for Mexico were augmented by other programs sponsored by North American firms that incorporated CIAA propaganda.

According to CIAA reports and surveys, the agency was able to disseminate its propaganda programs to a large percentage of the Mexican radio audience by means of network-produced recordings and programs created locally. By broadcasting programs in prime time several times a week over XEW—which had an estimated 75 percent share of the Mexico City radio audience, as well as significant audience shares in other central Mexican cities—CIAA propaganda consistently reached well over half of the available audience. The CIAA was able to achieve even larger audience shares by broadcasting a limited number of special programs in network with XEW, XEQ, and XEFO, as well as by broadcasting over other major Mexico City stations, including XEOY (Radio Mil) and XEB (CIAA, 1943–44, 1943e).

José Luis Ortiz Garza argues that Azcárraga and the CIAA had a perfect partnership throughout the war years (Ortiz Garza, 1989). It was a partnership based on the CIAA's recognition that XEW had "almost a monopoly of the radio audience and radio advertisers" in Mexico and could thus offer the CIAA a single, centralized means of access to the majority of the Mexican radio audience (Francisco, 1943:5). In exchange for this level of access, Azcárraga was well paid by the CIAA and rewarded with improved access to broadcasting equipment and expertise from the United States. Although Cerwin later claimed that the CIAA organized and financed Azcárraga's company, Radio Programas de Mexico, in 1941 and created "the first radio network in Mexico," Azcárraga seems to have been firmly in control of domestic broadcasting (Cerwin, 1966:206). Indeed, the CIAA was careful not to challenge Azcárraga's hegemony in Mexican broadcasting or do anything to jeopardize its privileged relationship with his organization.

Two examples are sufficient to illustrate the CIAA's cautious treatment of Azcárraga, particularly when it came to the issue of contracting with other stations to deliver CIAA programs. First, when well-financed Radio Mil (XEOY) broke into the Mexico City market with a sports-oriented program schedule, the CIAA moved cautiously to establish relations with the station. Francisco reported at the time that "radio XEOY faces very severe competition from XEW in getting commercial programs. XEW has by far the largest audience and threatens to put off its station or network any advertiser who uses a competing station. It is not known whether this is a bluff or fact but the threat is effective. Recently, when XEOY sold the broadcast of the bullfights to Coca-Cola, the arrangement was made practically subject to approval by Azcárraga, according to XEOY officials. In view of all the factors, it seemed desirable to me to help and encourage XEOY in every possible way that would not give offense to Azcárraga" (Francisco, 1943:9). While the CIAA was anxious to build relations with stations that would effectively deliver propaganda to the Mexican public, many of its actions also appeared to be "subject to approval by Azcárraga."

In another case, NBC was approached by the directors of the Mexico City network Cadena Radio Continental (CRC), who desired to form "a third international network in Latin America" with NBC's Blue Network. One CRC director stated that he wanted the Blue Network to send him American music, especially the "name bands," and expressed an interest in a direct telephone line connection to the NBC network. NBC declined, however, deferring to Azcárraga, who advised the network to "steer clear" of this organization. According to CRC promotional material, this upstart network was willing to use more North American–style programs and music than Azcárraga would have considered using over his established radio organization (CRC, n.d.; Rubio, 1942–43). Had the CIAA supported this alternative station it might have changed the balance of Mexican broadcasting—pushing it further toward a North American cultural model. The decision to follow the policies of the Azcárraga organization, then, limited the kinds of programs that the CIAA could disseminate in Mexico. Although the CIAA and U.S. networks ultimately held a great deal of indirect power in Mexican broadcasting because of their influence with North American advertisers and equipment dealers (as Azcárraga was well aware), in practice they chose to work through, not against, his well-positioned radio organization.

Program Content

While a detailed discussion of CIAA program development is beyond the scope of this work, it is important to point out the extent to which CIAA officials drew their program ideas from the U.S. broadcasting context. In particular, the agency's emphasis on dramatic narratives reflected the conviction of North American broadcasters that dramatic programs were the best means of getting and holding a radio audience (Vogel, 1943). These programs, dramatizing the heroic efforts of North Americans and Latin Americans alike to foil the Axis and catch Nazi spies, were transferred to the Mexican radio market, where very few dramatic narratives were broadcast in prime time. Along with dramatic programs, the CIAA also emphasized news commentary programs and dramatized news programs —models also borrowed from the North American context. CIAA officials also believed that broadcasts of American popular music would be an effective means of reaching Latin America's "farmers, peasants, common laborers, petty clerks, [and] small factory workers who prefer their messages presented to them in a light manner, rather than with very strong solid talk" (Vogel, 1943:2).

Given these expectations, CIAA administrators were surprised by the results of their audience surveys. The CIAA's Mexico committee conducted three surveys of Mexico City radio listeners between March 1943 and January 1944 using the "portable radio" method (see Chapter 1). Each survey worker covered a different neighborhood route during the prime-time evening hours of 7:00 P.M. to 10:15 P.M. In all, these surveys sampled more than 100,000 radios in what the committee believed was a representative sample of Federal District neighborhoods (see Figure 7.1). Although the surveys were conducted without the consent or knowledge of the Mexico City public, they offer extensive and relatively reliable information on the program preferences of Mexico City radio listeners in the early 1940s (Cerwin, 1943; CIAA, 1943–44, 1943e).[4]

The surveys consistently showed that *El hit parade*, a program of popular U.S. music produced by CBS and broadcast over station XEQ, received almost the lowest audience share of all CIAA programs broadcast in Mexico City (less than 7 percent of the listening audience) (CIAA, 1943–44). Although CIAA researchers failed to consider this fact carefully, *El hit parade*'s low rating was largely the result of the small audience share regularly garnered by station XEQ. Indeed, the CIAA survey found that XEQ averaged only a 7.24 audience share for all of its surveyed programs, which suggests that the hit music program's rating was roughly average for pro-

Figure 7.1 CIAA survey workers pose in front of a map of Mexico City. (Photo by Andrée Vilas; CIAA Central Files, box 346, folder "Surveys," April 14, 1943, RG 229, U.S. National Archives, College Park, Md.)

grams transmitted over station XEQ (CIAA, 1943e:2). Thus, *El hit parade* cannot be conclusively described as an "unpopular" program (although its rating was low compared with even the lowest rating received by a program broadcast over station XEW). CIAA officials, however, made precisely this interpretation of their findings: "A disappointment is the poor showing made by Hit Parade. This can only be explained by the fact that only a limited number of Mexicans, the younger ones, prefer American music to their own. Or can it be that the music of Hit Parade is so new that it reaches an unfamiliar and, therefore, an unresponsive ear? Or is it that the name Hit Parade is not understood by the people?" (CIAA, 1943e:8). Although officials considered finding a Spanish name for the program or switching it to station XEW in order to improve its ratings, reports continued to refer to the program as an unsuccessful effort to reach the Mexican audience (CIAA, 1943d:2). This erroneous conclusion appears to have influenced the CIAA's programming strategy. For example, committee officials decided not to move *El hit parade* to station XEW because they were convinced that it would not gain a significantly larger audience. *El hit parade* appears to have been the only regular program of North American popular music produced for Latin America by the CIAA.

The conclusion that American music was unpopular in Mexico City was also influenced by the committee's finding that the most popular programs on station XEW were musical variety programs featuring Mexican performances of predominantly Mexican music (CIAA, 1943e). Following this logic, the CIAA found that its programs reached the largest audience when they used a Mexican music and variety program format. For example, the CIAA program *Rapsodia panamericana*, featuring top Mexican musical and comedic talent, received an audience share of 76.92 percent when it was broadcast in network by XEW and XEQ (CIAA, 1943e). In addition, the CIAA found that the high ratings many of its programs received on station XEW were largely a by-product of the popularity of the Mexican musical programs they followed or preceded. This appears to have been the case with numerous CIAA programs, including *Mexican Interpretation of the War* (*Interpretación mexicana de la guerra*), *Tribute of Liberty* (*Tribuna de la libertad*), *The Truth Is* (*La verdad es*), and *The March of Time*. In his evaluation of the first Mexico City survey, radio expert Walter Krause noted that "March of Time may be our best show on the air for Mexico City but it seems to lose a great deal of the listening audience when it is broadcast" (Krause, 1943). Although the program reached 58.4 percent of the XEW listening audience, the preceding program garnered a 74.4 percent share, and the show after it had a 76 percent share. Krause concluded that "if sandwiching our programs between popular offerings is the only way we can keep an audience, it seems our programs cannot be considered popular" (Krause, 1943).

A comparison of CIAA programming objectives and audience survey results offers a view of the ways the CIAA was forced to package its message to fit the Mexican radio market. The author of the CIAA's second audience survey concluded that "after reviewing the results of this second survey, it appears evident that listeners in the Federal District want above all variety programs, with their own type of music and, if possible, comedy spots" (CIAA, 1943e:5). CIAA researchers found that Mexico City broadcasters had developed a distinct programming content in which North American–style programs did not easily fit. Indeed, they concluded

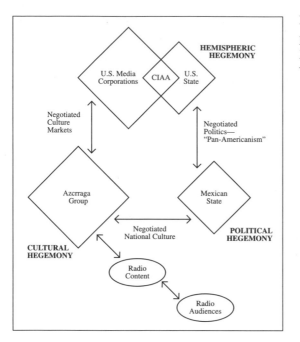

Figure 7.2 A model of power relations in Mexican radio during World War II.

that few, if any, CIAA programs could be considered truly "popular" with Mexican listeners.

Although the Mexican state certainly gave initial approval for the U.S. government's wartime propaganda initiative, it is striking that CIAA and NBC documents generally address Azcárraga as the chief negotiator for broadcasting activities in Mexico. The Mexican government clearly did not disappear from wartime broadcasting, and in fact added a *Military Hour* program to be broadcast by all Mexican stations along with the required *National Hour* program. In addition, Mexican presidential broadcasting was ubiquitous during the war years. Nonetheless, the lack of negotiations between the CIAA and representatives of the Mexican government suggests that a particular set of power relations had developed in Mexican broadcasting. By the early 1940s the Azcárraga organization had become the de facto representative of Mexican national interests in the sphere of broadcasting and popular culture more broadly (see Figure 7.2).

The CIAA's decision to use the Azcárraga organization to reach the largest possible Mexican audience kept it from building alternative broadcasting strategies in Mexico. The agency failed to support Cadena Radio Continental, for example, a network that was willing to experiment with a North American program content, including music. Instead, the CIAA and U.S. radio interests made concessions not only to the Azcárraga organization, but also to a programming content and style that had been developing in Mexico over the course of the 1930s: a musical content of commercialized Mexican and Latin American popular songs performed almost exclusively by Mexican performers. In the end, the CIAA strengthened the bond between Mexican popular culture and the broadcasting market that had been forged over the 1930s.

By choosing to broadcast through the Azcárraga organization and within the cultural boundaries of the Mexican broadcasting system, the CIAA chose to harness its message of "Americanism" to a broadcasting content of "Mexicanized" music and popular culture. In this the CIAA followed the practices of North American advertisers in Mexico who learned to work through Azcárraga's successful Mexican formula. Indeed, a 1947 article on advertising in Mexico reiterated the findings of the CIAA radio survey: to reach the Mexican audience advertisers had to conform to the Mexican broadcasting market, whose listeners preferred Mexico's "own music, emanating from its folk songs—the boleros, corridos, *tristes* and rancheros [*sic*]" (Thornburn, 1947:30). By the end of war, many U.S. officials, broadcasters, and advertisers were convinced that Mexican audiences preferred their own musical styles along with distinctly Mexican versions of serial dramas, game shows, and news programs (Jablons, 1949). The experiments, outcomes, and assumptions of the war years significantly shaped the postwar history of broadcasting in Mexico and Latin America as a whole.

Conclusion

Radio and Television in the Postwar Period

At the end of the twentieth century radio continued to have the widest reach and greatest penetration of any mass medium in Mexico,[1] although television had clearly displaced it as the central, nationwide broadcasting medium. Indeed, the postwar story of broadcasting is primarily the story of television rather than radio. Nonetheless, the development of radio broadcasting during the 1930s and 1940s fundamentally shaped the history of Mexican television. Key structural aspects of television broadcasting were in place by the early postwar period—well before the takeoff of television itself. These structural features included the hegemony of the Azcárraga Group and the particular regulatory framework of Mexican broadcasting. Thus radio laid the groundwork for television's role as the primary broadcasting medium and central site for the articulation of national culture. By way of television, then, Mexico remained a radio nation.

The Hegemony of the Azcárraga Group

There is no question that Emilio Azcárraga benefited greatly from his relationship with U.S. radio networks and the Office of the Coordinator of Inter-American Affairs (CIAA) during World War II. Although the war years witnessed enormous growth and development in Mexican broadcasting as a whole, including the rise of a half dozen national radio networks, the Azcárraga organization made the largest gains. While expanding domestically, Azcárraga also worked to internationalize his organization. By the end of the war, Radio Programas de México had thirty affiliated stations in Central America, the Caribbean, and South America; by the mid-1950s the number had grown to eighty affiliates in the region. Azcárraga signaled the preeminence of his broadcasting organization in 1948 with the construction of his massive Radiópolis (later Televicentro) headquarters in Mexico City (Hayes and McSherry, 1997).

Azcárraga's hegemonic position was firm enough to withstand two important challenges made during the war and early postwar periods. In both cases, these challenges were organized and aided by Mexican presidents with interests in broadcasting. As mentioned in Chapter 6, President Ávila Camacho had close connections to broadcasting through two ambitious figures: his campaign adviser, Alonso Sordo Noriega, and his brother, Secretary of Communications and Transport Maximino Ávila Camacho. Sordo Noriega was a talented announcer who dreamed of building a second broadcasting empire in Mexico with the president's help (Mejía Prieto, 1972). As early as 1942 he endeavored to purchase the powerful transmitter formerly owned by border blaster and radio quack Dr. John R. Brinkley (border blasters were North American–owned, English-language stations that broadcast to audiences in the United States from Mexican territory).[2] He planned to relocate the station to Mexico City and compete directly with Azcárraga. Sordo Noriega told a CIAA official that he "intended to set up a new radio station in Mexico and establish a chain of stations in Mexico that would make the XEW and XEQ stations look insignificant" (Ray, 1942). Indeed, in late 1943 the communications secretary opened up a prime broadcasting frequency for Sordo Noriega's station by moving Azcárraga's second flagship station, XEQ, from its preferred location at 730 kilocycles to 940 kilocycles (U.S. State Department, 1944).

Although Azcárraga anticipated competition from the new station as early as 1944, it was not up and running until October 1947, perhaps due to equipment and funding shortages (Ray, 1944). From the beginning, station XEX—"The Voice of Mexico" (La Voz de México)—was closely tied to the central government. Sordo Noriega was named general manager, and funding for the station came in part from the government's oil corporation, PEMEX. The station was constructed on the outskirts of Mexico City on ranch land reportedly owned by ex-president Ávila Camacho, suggesting another possible source of funding. Transmitting on XEQ's old frequency with 250 kilowatts of power, XEX surpassed XEW as the hemisphere's most powerful station (Riggs, 1947; Mejía Prieto, 1972). The station also reflected President Alemán's socially conservative vision for a "new" Mexico. In his inaugural broadcast, Sordo Noriega announced the station's goal to present "decent" and "moral" radio programs: "We want to enter the homes of Mexico with an accent of dignity and decency, banishing all degenerate things [*lo innoble*] that might stain the purity of our children or the modesty of our wives" (Mejía Prieto, 1972:80). With this philosophy, station XEX was poised to help rebuild the moral fabric of the nation by celebrating Christian morality, patriarchal authority, and the sanctity of the middle-class home.

At his untimely death in 1949, however, Sordo Noriega had failed to realize his dream. Although XEX became a significant presence in Mexican broadcasting, the enterprise could not seriously rival Azcárraga's empire without enormous financial backing from private investors. Nonetheless, station XEX became part of another, more serious postwar challenge to the Azcárraga Group. According to Alex Saragoza, Azcárraga's initial bid for a television broadcasting concession was rejected in 1946 by President Ávila Camacho and President-elect Alemán (Saragoza, 1997). Like Sordo Noriega, Alemán had a dream of a second broadcasting empire in Mexico, but he was much better equipped to make that dream a reality. Once he became president, Alemán persuaded Mexican businessman Rómulo O'Farrill, who had made his fortune in the automobile business, to enter the media industry—first through the newspaper *Novedades*, and then through station XEX. O'Farrill received the first television broadcasting concession in 1949, and Alemán became a personal investor in the new medium.

Although Azcárraga received the second television concession just a year later, he faced serious competition from the well-financed O'Farrill organization. In the end, however, after years of expensive competition, it was O'Farrill who approached Azcárraga about the possibility of a merger, and Azcárraga who clearly held the upper hand in the corporation they formed in 1955: Telesistema Mexicano. When another competing group surfaced more than a decade later, Azcárraga was also able to dominate the corporate product of their 1972 merger: Televisa. Even in the face of well-financed competitors, Azcárraga's formula of market nationalism and government cooperation ensured his hegemony from World War II through the 1990s. Although the Azcárraga Group faced increasing challenges from broadcasting, cable, and other media ventures, as late as 1995 Televisa continued to hold an 80 percent share of the Mexican television audience (Malkin and Landler, 1994; Malkin, 1997; Saragoza, 1997).

Thus, the trajectory of television development can be traced directly to the rise of Azcárraga's radio empire in the years before World War II. Like Brazil, Mexico developed a single television conglomerate that dominated not only nationally but regionally. Cuba would probably have developed a similar system had it not been for the country's socialist revolution (Salwen, 1994). In all three cases, television development was predicated on the existence of massive radio broadcasting enterprises that drew on a domestic content that seemed to be ready-made for radio: popular music. Cuba's bolero, rumba, and mambo; Brazil's samba; and Mexico's canción and ranchera laid the foundation for radio broadcasting in these countries. As a visual medium, however, television could not make the same central use of these musical forms. Although television broadcasters had access to a large body of Mexican films, these were not especially suited to the flow and form of the new medium and they could not begin to fill its ravenous appetite. After experimenting with live dramatic forms, television broadcasters came to rely on program formats adapted from radio, especially the variety show (including generous amounts of popular music), the game show, and the telenovela (Jacobs, 1951).

Despite the competition of cheap television programs from the United States beginning in the late 1960s, Mexico's most popular television stations offered predominantly Mexican-made programs. Indeed, surveys in the 1980s and 1990s found that Latin American television audiences in general preferred nationally produced programs, followed by programs from other Latin American countries; programs from the United States came in last (Antola and Rogers, 1984; Straubhaar, 1991; McAnany and La Pastina, 1994).

By the early 1980s both Mexico and Brazil were major program exporters to other Latin American countries, as well as to Spanish-language broadcasters in the United States (Gutiérrez and Reina Schement, 1984; Rodriguez, 1996; Saragoza, 1997). In both countries, the creation of national television conglomerates was based on a similar formula: a large market capable of sustaining an independent broadcasting system, a history of state repression and close state-industry cooperation, and media entrepreneurs with the resources and creativity to develop local cultural forms and adapt foreign forms to the national market (Oliveira, 1993). In the case of Mexico, all of this began in radio.

Broadcasting Regulations

Television's regulatory regime was also adapted from radio. Indeed, as early as 1942 the two key forces that would shape television regulation were in place: the official industry organization, the Radio Industry Chamber (the CIR, later CIRT); and the state's regulatory framework for radio. Under the influence of Mexico's most prominent commercial broadcasters—including key members of the Azcárraga Group—the CIR developed close and cooperative relations with the central government. This style of cooperation would continue through the television era. In addition, the CIR developed and promoted its own national and regional regulatory agenda. In 1946 members of the CIR organized the Inter-American Association of Radio Broadcasters (Asociación Inter-Americana de Radiodifusoras; AIR) to unify and codify broadcasting legislation throughout the region. In 1948 the AIR drew up a series of principles to guide broadcasting regulations, with a particular eye to the commercial development of the television medium. These principles characterized broadcasting as a private activity undertaken in the public interest (rather than a public service in itself) and declared that the state should limit its regulations to the technical aspects of broadcasting and stay out of direct competition with commercial broadcasters. Through the lobbying of the CIRT, these principles fundamentally shaped television regulations in Mexico (Mejía Barquera, 1989; Hayes and McSherry, 1997).

Codification of television regulations, however, was relatively slow. During the medium's first ten years no major new regulation was enacted, and television developed under the framework of the 1942 broadcasting law, or Reglamento. Although the 1942 law was more permissive than previous regulations for non-Spanish-language broadcasts (primarily commercials and recorded programs from the United States), it maintained the nationalistic structure of the system and continued to require each station to include at least 25 percent "typically Mexican music" in its broadcast schedule

(Leyva, 1992:144). When the Federal Law of Radio and Television (LFRT) was finally passed in 1960, it continued many of these nationalistic requirements; however, it also reflected the CIRT's efforts to liberalize the regulatory regime. Specifically, the LFRT implemented the key principles formulated by the AIR in 1948 by declaring broadcasting a private activity and reducing the state's control over broadcasting content (Mejía Barquera, 1989).

The 1960 LFRT shaped the development of Mexican television through the 1990s. Although the requirement that broadcasters promote national culture was significantly diluted, concessionaires were still required to ensure that at least 30 percent of their broadcast day was filled with programs of Mexican origin. While nationalistic regulations declined somewhat in the 1970s (for example, the required percentage of Mexican-origin programs was reduced to 10 percent), the state's visibility in broadcasting increased considerably. First, the state regenerated its role as a broadcaster in its own right with the opening of the SEP's Radio Educación station, XEEP, in 1967. Later ventures would continue the state's role as both a radio and television broadcaster. Second, the state became a significant presence in commercial broadcasting through a 1969 agreement that apportioned control of more than 12.5 percent of the broadcast day to the central government in exchange for the withdrawal of a proposed tax on broadcasting services. The state used these hours of commercial airtime to promote its developmental and economic policies, celebrate its vision of national culture, and solidify the political hegemony of the Partido Revolucionario Institucional (PRI, the state's official party) (Hayes and McSherry, 1997).

In sum, television regulations did not depart significantly from the radio regulations forged through decades of state-industry negotiation. If anything, the LFRT gave both parties more of what they wanted without regard for the broader social or public interest. Commercial broadcasters gained more latitude to exploit the medium for profit, and the state gained an even greater and more exclusive presence in civil society.

Radio's Transformation

Radio's transformation from a primary to a secondary broadcast medium was a slow one in Mexico for several reasons. First, the penetration of television technology was slow. Only 17 percent of the population had access to the new medium in 1965 (assuming six people per television set), 35 percent in 1970, and 65 percent in 1985 (Wilkie and Contreras, 1992). Second, despite the flight of talent and capital from radio to television, radio broadcasting continued to grow and consolidate. As discussed above, Azcárraga continued to build his AM radio empire during the 1950s and 1960s, and he was joined in the radio market by a number of new radio networks and operating groups. In addition, as Mexico's population grew, so did the available radio audience. The number of radio receivers increased from about three million in the late 1950s to more than fourteen million by 1970. As late as 1977 almost 30 percent of Mexican radio stations were still broadcasting radionovelas, suggesting the continuation of radio's classic formats well into the television era (Hayes and McSherry, 1997).

In general, radio's post-television transformation was shaped by two contradictory developments. First, radio programming shifted from a national to a local or regional focus. In part, this change reflected the enormous multiplication of radio stations—from about three hundred at the end of the 1950s to almost two thousand in the mid-1990s. With more stations on the air and growing competition from television, commercial broadcasters diversified their radio formats to target specific audience markets. While popular music still dominated radio content, genre-specific music formats (such as *tropical* or *grupero*) were developed to further differentiate available markets. News, sports, and talk-radio formats also proliferated. In addition, there was a large influx of noncommercial broadcasters (some state sponsored) during the 1980s and 1990s who aimed to reach particular social groups (students, indigenous groups) through more localized, "narrow-casting" strategies (Romo, 1990; Hayes and McSherry, 1997). Another important phenomenon was the rise of talk radio in the urban environment as an increasingly open forum for social, cultural, and political debate (Quiñones, 1996; Zamba, 1996; García Canclini, 1998; Winocur, 1998; Pannaralla, 1999).

At the same time, however, the radio industry as a whole continued its trend toward centralization and concentration of both ownership and programming strategies. Although new broadcasting chains regularly entered the market beginning in the 1960s, the overall structure of the industry remained highly concentrated. In the 1960s, 20 percent of broadcasters accounted for about 68 percent of industry income, and by the 1970s, 61 percent of all stations were in the hands of six major consortia. This situation continued in the following decades: in the 1980s, fifteen groups controlled 80 percent of all stations, and in the 1990s, the majority of stations were owned by the ten largest consortia. Consolidation strategies were also aided by the use of satellite technologies that provided a new means of integrating and standardizing the national radio market. For example, Grupo ACIR, a major broadcasting conglomerate, used satellite uplinks to transmit radio programs to affiliated stations in more than sixty Mexican cities every day. Through national radio news programs such as Radio Red's *Monitor*, radio continued to provide centralized program content for a nationwide audience (Fernández Christleib, 1991; Hayes and McSherry, 1997).

Despite the proliferation of commercial and noncommercial radio stations, both the format and the economics of the medium continued to demand centralization and repetition of content. As discussed in Chapter 2, radio's constant flow consumes such quantities of programming content that even small, community-oriented stations must rely on prerecorded programming created by large-scale, centralized producers. This has long been the case with recorded music, but it is also true of news and other kinds of public affairs programming. In addition, the concentration of stations and networks in the hands of a small group of broadcasters has not diminished with the rise of television or the multiplication of radio outlets. Indeed, concentration increased due to mergers and buyouts in the 1990s as broadcasters faced growing competition from other media (Hayes and McSherry, 1997). For these reasons, radio showed no signs of becoming a truly decentralized, local medium; instead, it continued to inundate increasingly fragmented national markets with increasingly standardized programming.

What was true for radio at the end of the twentieth century was doubly true for television: local stations relied on prerecorded programming produced by national and international television conglomerates. For example, a 1992 study found that less than 1 percent of 495 weekly hours of television in the city of Colima, Mexico, was locally produced (González, 1992). In a situation replicated in other parts of Mexico, almost 80 percent of those interviewed in the Colima study identified Televisa's Channel 2 as their favorite station. Although North American television programs dubbed into Mexican Spanish were widely available to Mexican broadcasters, Televisa's Channel 2 continued to broadcast 100 percent nationally produced programs (González, 1992). The expense of producing television programs reduced the possibility that programs would be produced locally at the same time that the domination of Televisa ensured that the medium would retain a distinctly national content. Although the consumption and interpretation of television programs remained radically local in the late 1990s, there is no question that the production of television—based on the radio model—remained national.

Reflections on a Radio Nation

This book set out to cover three main areas of historical terrain: the history of radio development, the history of nation formation, and the intersection of radio and nation in the arena of Mexican popular culture. In tracing the history of radio development, I have not attempted to distinguish between broadcasting as a technological form and broadcasting as a set of social practices. Indeed, I argue that radio's antimodern trajectory is a product of both its unique technology and the particular social uses of the medium. For example, radio's role in promoting antimodern forms of identity and authority was shaped by its sound format as well as by the particular programming strategies used by broadcasters. While the tactile quality of radio sound immersed listeners in an invisible collectivity, the program content of Mexican radio emphasized paternalist relations and nostalgic traditions. These strategies can be seen in both the practices of presidential radio speaking and the selective musical traditions developed by government and commercial radio broadcasters.

In approaching the history of nation formation in Mexico, I have focused on broadcasting as a social terrain in which "the national" is articulated, challenged, and negotiated. For example, from the very earliest laws and regulations, the Mexican broadcasting system was defined as a public resource coterminous with the Mexican nation. At the same time, however, Mexican broadcasting was fundamentally shaped by U.S. corporate and government interests that controlled both radio technology and the economic organization of the medium. The nation, then, is both a dominant social category and a negotiated reality. This is particularly clear in the case of Mexican broadcasting during World War II. In particular, the Azcárraga Group's unique role in wartime radio suggests the complex processes of negotiation through which competing interests construct and represent the nation as a social, cultural, and political forum.

Finally, this book investigates popular culture through a series of institutions and actors who attempted to mobilize it for particular social ends. As constructed by both government and commercial broadcasters, popular culture provided an ideal means of creating meaning in the unstable, shifting space of the modern nation and the rapid flow of the radio medium. Partly through its own mythology as a "vernacular" practice firmly tied to the particular place and time of its production, popular culture served to create both the "authenticity" of the nation and the unity of the radio audience. At the same time, however, the constant flow and recombination of popular culture reflected both the evanescence of radio broadcasting and the permeability of the modern nation. Ultimately, this book argues that Mexican popular culture cannot be viewed as an essential or authentic cultural product; it must instead be seen as a process of communication— a dialogue—between "local," "national," and "foreign" cultural practices. As a historically grounded and socially embodied communication practice, popular culture shapes and animates the Radio Nation.

Notes

Introduction

1. This book deals specifically with radio as a broadcasting technology rather than a form of point-to-point communication. Thus, *radio* and *broadcasting* are used interchangeably. In addition, I view radio as a social practice that combines and conflates at least four analytically separable elements: (1) broadcasting as a technology with particular sensory and organizational capacities; (2) the economic institutions of broadcasting; (3) broadcasting as a political forum; and (4) broadcasting as a set of cultural practices of production, distribution, and reception. A key characteristic of radio broadcasting is the way the elements act in concert to shape the medium's possibilities and limitations at any given time.

2. For this discussion I am indebted to Kathleen Newman (personal communication, March 24, 1999).

3. The official call letters were XEFX, though all documents give them as XFX.

Chapter 1. Radio, Nation, and Mexican History

1. This agency, created under the Council of National Defense, was initially called the Office of the Coordinator of Latin American Commercial and Cultural Relations. The name was shortened to Office of the Coordinator of Inter-American Affairs in August 1941. In other works this agency is abbreviated variously as CIAA, OCIAA, and OIAA. I use CIAA because this is the abbreviation used in the agency's own publications.

2. While battery-powered radios were available, their cost was prohibitive. In the pretransistor era, affordable radios required AC electricity.

3. For a more extensive discussion of changes in historical scholarship on the Mexican Revolution during the 1980s, see Vaughan, 1999.

Chapter 2. The Antimodern Trajectories of Radio and Nation

1. This sense of "unreality" was a product of rapid urbanization and industrialization, the growth of an immigrant working class, and the rise of monopoly capitalism.

2. L. J. Reynolds, personal communication, October 24, 1998.

3. Although scholars have explored the concept of flow most fully in the case of television, it has also been a key concept in radio history. Radio flow was first identified from the perspective of performers and producers who characterized the medium as a "ravenous maw" and "treadmill to oblivion."

4. Early radio researchers similarly found little difference between the way that listeners responded to live voices and the way they reacted to radio voices (Cantril and Allport, 1971).

Chapter 3. The Birth of Broadcasting

1. Luis Rivera-Perez provides a particularly insightful and comprehensive review of these theories and explores their influence on the work of Nestor García Canclini and Jesús Martín-Barbero. Other important contributions to this discussion can be found in Straubhaar, 1991; Tomlinson, 1992; Nordenstreng and Schiller, 1993; García Canclini, 1995; Chen, 1996; and Suvanandan, 1998–99.

2. In the United States during this period, the term *affiliate* denoted an independent, commercial radio station that was connected by telephone lines to a broadcasting network and which devoted almost all of its prime-time hours to network programs. Networks in the United States had no permanent telephone connections with Mexican stations and instead made only occasional shortwave transmissions or phone-line connections to Mexican "affiliates" for special-event broadcasts. Likewise, Mexican "networks" were not regularly connected by phone lines.

3. During the period known as the Maximato, Calles remained the controlling power behind the short-term presidents who succeeded him: Emilio Portes Gil (1928–30), Pascual Ortiz Rubio (1930–32), and Abelardo L. Rodríguez (1932–34).

4. These regulations were often open to negotiation by means of bribery and corruption, particularly in the U.S.-Mexico border region.

Chapter 4. Broadcasting the Revolution

1. Primary materials cited are from two different collections held at the Archivo Histórico de la SEP: the "Radio Educación" collection, including documents from the SEP Depto. de Bellas Artes, and the "Oficina Cultural Radiotelefónica" collection, from the SEP office of the same name. These papers include the internal memos, proposals, program schedules, and scripts relating to the operation of radio station XFX.

2. J. D. Andrew, personal communication, December 1998.

3. The OCR collection contains program schedules for March through December 1933. Some months were incomplete; in all, 135 daily schedules were examined.

Chapter 5. Nation as Market

1. Station XEB schedules (7:00 P.M. to 11:00 P.M.) were examined for the first Saturday and Wednesday of January, March, September, and November of each year. Radio Mil (XEOY) or XEX schedules were used if XEB schedules were not printed. Due to irregularities in printing, all schedules were not available. Year by year, the number of listings examined were: 1938, 8 XEB; 1940, 8 XEB; 1942, 3 XEB; 1944, 7 XEB, 1 XEOY; 1946, 6 XEB; 1948, 1 XEB, 1 XEOY, 2 XEX. A total of 37 days/148 hours of programming was examined.

Chapter 6. The Paternal Voice of the Nation

1. *Tata* means "dear father" in the indigenous Tarascan language.

2. The negative appraisal of Cárdenas's radio style was also confirmed by Ramón Eduardo Ruíz (personal communication, May 1991).

3. An examination of the first fifteen folders in this collection revealed two folders of letters sent in direct response to the speech (Legajo 1–2). I chose to limit my analysis to folder 1 because it included the most immediate responses, while not varying appreciably from the content of folder 2. The titles and contents of the other folders did not indicate the presence of more responses to the March 18 broadcast, although this cannot be ruled out entirely. Indeed, the reported level of public response suggests that many more telegrams were originally received.

4. This discussion owes a great deal to the astute observations of Ernesto Acevedo-Muñoz (personal communication, August 1997).

5. Although Krauze states that the play was written in 1938 and made its debut performance in 1947, Alexander Pineda and Paulo Antonio Paranaguá note that the play was performed in 1937 (Pineda and Paranaguá, 1995).

Chapter 7. Radio at War

1. World Wide Broadcasting, owned by Walter Lemmon, was funded principally by grants from the Rockefeller Foundation and later the CIAA. The station's objective was to "offer a standard for broadcasts to South and Central America, and to appeal, at the beginning, to the more cultured members of each community" (Rockefeller, 1937:7). The types of programs broadcast by World Wide's Boston station, WIXAL, included classical music, poetry, and dramatic readings by Latin America diplomats and literati, and what was described as a "general inter-American cultural program" (Rockefeller, 1938:10–11). Overall, the Rockefeller Foundation funded World Wide as part of a high-cultural and education-oriented radio "mission" to Latin America with the aim of building better relations between the United States and a cultural elite of Latin American listeners.

2. It is important to note that Mexico was never referred to as being part of North America in NBC and CIAA discussions of Latin American broadcasting. References to South and Central America were used to describe Latin America as a whole and should be understood to include Mexico.

3. Other factors influencing the newspapers were Mexican government pressure and the need for equipment and other printing supplies from the United States.

4. For a critique of CIAA survey methods, see Krause, 1943.

Conclusion

1. This chapter draws heavily on Hayes and McSherry, 1997.

2. The border blasters had a significant impact on North American radio broadcasting and U.S. culture more broadly beginning in the 1930s. For a history, see Fowler and Crawford, 1990; and Ortiz Garza, 1997.

References

Acevedo-Muñoz, E. R. 1998. "Deconstructing Nationalism: Luis Buñuel and the Crisis of Classical Mexican Cinema, 1946–1955." Ph.D. diss., University of Iowa.

Aitken, H.G.J. 1985. *The Continuous Wave: Technology and American Radio, 1900–1932*. Princeton: Princeton University Press.

Alexander, C. C. 1980. *Here the Country Lies: Nationalism and the Arts in Twentieth-Century America*. Bloomington: University of Indiana Press.

Alisky, M. 1954. "Early Mexican Broadcasting." *Hispanic American Historical Review* 34 (November): 513–26.

Altman, R. 1994. "Deep-Focus Sound: Citizen Kane and the Radio Aesthetic." *Quarterly Journal of Film and Video* 15 (3): 1–33.

Anderson, B. 1991. *Imagined Communities:Reflections on the Origin and Spread of Nationalism*. 2d ed. London: Verso.

Anthias, F., and N. Yuval-Davis, eds. 1989. *Woman-Nation-State*. London: Macmillan.

Antola, L., and E. M. Rogers. 1984. "Television Flows in Latin America." *Communication Research* 11 (2): 183–202.

Arnheim, R. 1936. *Radio*. Trans. Margaret Ludwig and Herbert Read. London: Faber and Faber.

Arredondo Ramírez, P., and E. E. Sánchez Ruíz. 1986. *Comunicación social, poder y democracia en México*. Guadalajara: University of Guadalajara.

Ávila Camacho, M. 1940. Address, December 31. Sound recording (RWB 5454 A3). Motion Picture, Broadcasting and Recorded Sound. Library of Congress, Washington, D.C.

Azcárraga, E. 1942. Letter to John Royal, June 3. Royal Papers, box 110, folder

"Royal—CIAA, 1942–44." The NBC Collection, Wisconsin State Historical Society, Madison.

Badillo, A. 1933. Letter to Narciso Bassols, April 29. Expediente 37, caja 1310. Oficina Cultural Radiotelefónica, Archivo Histórico de la SEP, Mexico City.

Baer, M. D. 1991. "Television and Political Control in Mexico." Ph.D. diss., University of Michigan, Ann Arbor.

Balibar, E. 1991. "Racism and Nationalism." In E. Balibar and I. Wallerstein, eds., *Race, Nation, Class: Ambiguous Identities* (pp. 37–67). London: Verso.

Barbour, P. L. 1940. "Commercial and Cultural Broadcasting in Mexico." *Annals of the American Academy of Political and Social Sciences* 108 (March): 94–102.

Barthes, R. 1977. *Image—Music—Text.* Trans. S. Heath. Glasgow: Fontana.

———. 1990. "The Grain of the Voice" (1977). In S. Firth and A. Goodwin, eds., *On Record: Rock, Pop, and the Written Word* (pp. 293–300). New York: Routledge.

Becker, M. 1995. *Setting the Virgin on Fire: Lázaro Cárdenas, Michoacán Peasants, and the Redemption of the Mexican Revolution.* Berkeley: University of California Press.

Bederman, G. 1995. *Manliness and Civilization: A Cultural History of Gender and Race in the United States, 1880–1917.* Chicago: University of Chicago Press.

Beezley, W. H., C. E. Martin, and W. E. French, eds. 1994. *Rituals of Rule, Rituals of Resistance.* Wilmington, Del.: SR Books.

Bellas Artes. 1932a. Estación de radio de la Secretaria de Educación, undated. Expediente 1068, Radio Educación. Depto. de Bellas Artes, Archivo Histórico de la SEP, Mexico City.

———. 1932b. "Obra de extensión educativa por radio," undated. Expediente 1068, Radio Educación. Depto. de Bellas Artes, Archivo Histórico de la SEP, Mexico City.

———. 1932c. "Proyecto de un programa de trabajo . . . ," undated. Expediente 1068, Radio Educación. Depto. de Bellas Artes, Archivo Histórico de la SEP, Mexico City.

———. 1932d. Untitled report, undated. Expediente 1068, Radio Educación. Depto. de Bellas Artes, Archivo Histórico de la SEP, Mexico City.

Benjamin, W. 1993. "Theater and Radio: Toward the Mutual Control of Their Work of Instruction (1931/32)." In N. Strauss, ed., *Radiotext(e)* (pp. 29–31). New York: Columbia University Press.

Blanco, J. J. 1982. "Cultura nacional y cultura de estado." *Cuadernos políticos* 34 (October–December): 75–84.

Booth, G. C. 1941. *Mexico's School-Made Society.* California: Stanford University Press.

Bourdon, J. 1998. "The Early Americanisation of European Television. 'America' as a Professional Resource." Paper presented at the "Media History?" Conference, London.

Bowles, P. 1940–41. "On Mexico's Popular Music." *Modern Music* 18 (November–June): 225–30.

Bracker, Milton. 1946. "Shift to Right Is Seen for Mexico." *New York Times*, December 16, p. 14.

Brading, D. A. 1985. *The Origins of Mexican Nationalism.* Cambridge: Cambridge University Press.

Brenner, A. 1948. "Mexico's New Deal Two Years After." *New York Times Magazine*, November 28, p. 19.

Breuilly, J. 1982. *Nationalism and the State.* Manchester: University of Manchester Press.

Brewer, A. 1990. *Marxist Theories of Imperialism: A Critical Survey.* 2d ed. London and New York: Routledge.

Britton, J. A. 1971. "The Mexican Ministry of Education, 1931–1940: Radical and Institutional Development." Ph.D. diss., Tulane University.

Brunk, S. 1998. "Remembering Emiliano Zapata: Three Moments in the Posthumous Career of the Martyr of Cinameca." *Hispanic American Historical Review* 78 (3): 457–90.

Cadena Radio Continental [CRC]. n.d. Brochure. Miscellaneous Reports and Issuances, 1941–43, box 965. CIAA, RG 229, U.S. National Archives, College Park, Md.

Cantril, H., and G. W. Allport. 1971. *The Psychology of Radio.* 1935. Reprint. New York: Arno Press.

Cárdenas, L. 1936. "Declaración del motivos por el cual se crea el DAPP," undated. Expediente 545.2/33. Ramo Presidente, gal. 3. Archivo General de la Nación, Mexico City.

———. 1938. Felicitaciones Asunto Petrolero 18 y 19 de Marzo. Legajo 1. Expediente 432.2/253-1. Ramo Presidente, gal. 3. Archivo General de la Nación, Mexico City.

———. 1940. *¡Cárdenas habla!* Mexico City: Partido Revolucionario Mexicano.

———. 1978. *Palabras y documentos públicos de Lázaro Cárdenas, 1928-1970.* Vol. 1 (1928-1940). Mexico City: Siglo Veintiuno Editores.

Cardoso, F. H. 1972. "Dependency and Development in Latin America." *New Left Review* 74 (July–August): 83–95.

Carr, B. 1994. "The Fate of the Vanguard under a Revolutionary State: Marxism's Contribution to the Construction of the Great Arch." In G. M. Joseph and D. Nugent, eds., *Everyday Forms of State Formation: Revolution and the Negotia-*

tion of Rule in Modern Mexico (pp. 326–52). Durham and London: Duke University Press.

CBS. 1941. "CBS Forges Another Station Link in Its 'Network of the Americas' . . . July 10." Press release. Royal Papers, box 112, folder "Royal Short Wave . . . Contracts, 1941–44." The NBC Collection, Wisconsin State Historical Society, Madison.

Cerwin, H. 1942. Memo to Nelson A. Rockefeller, October 14. Central Files, box 345, folder "Mexico." CIAA, RG 229, U.S. National Archives, College Park, Md.

———. 1943. Memo to Nelson A. Rockefeller, July 1. Attn. Francisco, Re: Survey. Central Files, box 347, folder "Surveys." CIAA, RG 229, U.S. National Archives, College Park, Md.

———. 1966. *In Search of Something: The Memoirs of a Public Relations Man.* Los Angeles: Sherbourne Press.

Chatterjee, P. 1993a. *The Nation and Its Fragments: Colonial and Post-colonial Histories.* Princeton: Princeton University Press.

———. 1993b. *Nationalist Thought and the Colonial World: A Derivative Discourse.* 1986. Reprint. Minneapolis: University of Minnesota Press.

Chávez, C. 1945. "Music in a Mexican Test Tube." *New York Times Magazine,* July 2, p. 8.

Chen, K.-H. 1996. "Not Yet the Postcolonial Era: The (Super) Nation-State and Transnationalism of Cultural Studies: Response to Ang and Stratton." *Cultural Studies* 10 (1): 37–70.

Clark, K. 1969. *Civilization: A Personal View.* New York: Harper and Row.

Coordinator of Inter-American Affairs [CIAA]. 1942a. "A 'Don' from the U.S." Clipping. San Francisco Office, General Records, box 973, folder "Don Francisco." CIAA, RG 229, U.S. National Archives, College Park, Md.

———. 1942b. "History of the CIAA," November 1. Entry 2, box 512. CIAA, RG 229, U.S. National Archives, College Park, Md.

———. 1942c. "Resume of Commercial Cooperation for Field Manual," October 16. Central Files, box 240, folder "Radio Manual," CIAA, RG 229, U.S. National Archives, College Park, Md.

———. 1943–44. "Third Radio Survey of Mexico, D.F., December 27–January 30." Central Files, box 347. CIAA, RG 229, U.S. National Archives, College Park, Md.

———. 1943a. "Activities of the CIAA in the Other Republics." Unpublished report. Central Files, box 513. CIAA, RG 229, U.S. National Archives, College Park, Md.

———. 1943b. "Changes in Information Program," January 11. Miscellaneous Records, box 1459, folder "Content Directives . . . Duggan Themes," CIAA, RG 229, U.S. National Archives, College Park, Md.

———. 1943c. "Information Directives," April. Miscellaneous Records, box 1459, folder "Content Directives Long Range," CIAA, RG 229, U.S. National Archives, College Park, Md.

———. 1943d. "Radio Survey of Seven Interior Cities," April 14–June 30. Miscellaneous Reports and Issuances, 1941–43, box 965. CIAA, RG 229, U.S. National Archives, College Park, Md.

———. 1943e. "Second Radio Survey of Mexico, D.F.," July 12–35; August 16–22; August 30–September 12. Miscellaneous Reports and Issuances, 1941–43, box 965. CIAA, RG 229, U.S. National Archives, College Park, Md.

———. 1944. "General Directives—for the Information Program of the American Association," December 11. Central Files, box 342, folder "Operating Procedures," CIAA, RG 229, U.S. National Archives, College Park, Md.

———. 1946a. "A History of the CIAA," undated. Entry 2, box 512. CIAA, RG 229, U.S. National Archives, College Park, Md.

———. 1946b. *A History of the Office of the Coordinator of Inter-American Affairs.* Washington, D.C.: Government Printing Office.

———. 1947. *History of the Office of the Coordinator of Inter-American Affairs.* Washington, D.C.: Government Printing Office.

Crisell, A. 1994. *Understanding Radio.* 2d ed. London: Routledge.

Culturas Populares, Museo Nacional de. 1984. *El pais de las tandas: Teatro de revista, 1900–1940.* Coyoacan: Museo Nacional de Culturas Populares.

De Grazia, V. 1992. *How Fascism Ruled Women, Italy, 1922–1945.* Berkeley: University of California Press.

Deihl, E. R. 1977. "South of the Border: The NBC and CBS Radio Networks and the Latin American Venture, 1930–1942." *Communication Quarterly* 25 (4): 2–12.

Deutsch, K. W. 1967. "Nation and World." In I. de S. Pool, ed., *Contemporary Political Science: Toward Empirical Theory* (pp. 204–27). New York: McGraw-Hill, 1967.

Duara, P. 1995. *Rescuing History from the Nation: Questioning Narratives of Modern China.* Chicago: University of Chicago Press.

Edwards, D. 1997. "Flow and the Political Economy of the Super Text." Ph.D. diss., University of Texas, Austin.

El Machete. 1931. "La voz del Partido Comunista de México desde la 'X.E.W.'" *El Machete*, November 10 and 20.

El Universal. 1947. "El hogar mexicano es la patria misma." *El Universal,* January 1, p. 1.

———. 1950. "Fe en el trabajo y confianza en Mexico pide el señor presidente." *El Universal,* January 1, pp. 1, 7.

Encyclopedia de México. 1987. "Mauricio Magdaleno" and "Rudolfo Usigli." Mexico City: Secretaría de Educación Pública.

Estrada, J., ed. 1984. *La música de México, historia, período nacionalista (1910 a 1958).* Mexico City: UNAM.

Excelsior. 1934a. "Niñez y juventud deben ser para la revolución." *Excelsior,* July 21, pp. 1, 3.

———. 1934b. "Un mensaje del Gral. Cárdenas a los obreros." *Excelsior,* May 3, pp. 3–4.

———. 1936. "Un vasto plan de reconstrucción nacional realizará el ejecutivo. *Excelsior,* January 2, pp. 1–3.

———. 1937. "Habla por radio el C. presidente." *Excelsior,* January 2, pp. 1–3.

———. 1938. Mensaje del presidente de la república a la nación. *Excelsior,* January 2, pp. 1–7.

———. 1944. Mensaje de optimismo del presidente a la nación. *Excelsior,* January 1, pp. 1–2.

———. 1945. La política subterránea nulifica la obra constructiva del país. *Excelsior,* January 1, pp. 1.

Farmer, E. M. 1996. "Backwards and Forwards: A Review of Five Recent Works on Mexico." *Historical Journal* 39 (4): 1127–35.

Fejes, F. 1981. "Media Imperialism: An Assessment." *Media, Culture, and Society* 3:281–89.

———. 1986. *Imperialism, Media, and the Good Neighbor: New Deal Foreign Policy and United States Shortwave Broadcasting to Latin America.* Norwood, N.J.: Ablex.

Fernández Christlieb, F. 1985. *Los medios de difusión masiva en México.* Mexico City: Juan Pablos Editor.

———. 1991. *La radio mexicana: Centro y regiones.* Mexico City: Juan Pablos.

Fowler, G., and B. Crawford. 1990. *Border Radio: Quacks, Yodelers, Pitchmen, Psychics, and Other Amazing Broadcasters of the American Airwaves.* 1987. Reprint. New York: Limelight Editions.

Fox, E. 1997. *Latin American Broadcasting: From Tango to Telenovela.* Luton, England: University of Luton Press.

Francisco, D. 1942. Letter to James R. Woodul, September 4. Central Files, box 343, folder "Mexico Programs—Rebroadcast," CIAA, RG 229, U.S. National Archives, College Park, Md.

―――. 1943. "Field Inspection Report on Mexico, May 10–17." Miscellaneous Reports and Issuances, 1941–43, box 964, folder "Reports—Field Inspection, Mexico," CIAA, RG 229, U.S. National Archives, College Park, Md.

Frank, A. G. 1969. *Capitalism and Underdevelopment in Latin America: Historical Studies of Chile and Brazil.* New York: Monthly Review Press.

Frischmann, D. H. 1994. "Misiones Culturales, Teatro Conasupo, and Teatro Communidad: The Evolution of Rural Theater." In W. H. Beezley, C. E. Martin, and W. E. French, eds., *Rituals of Rule, Rituals of Resistance* (pp. 285–306). Wilmington, Del.: SR Books.

García Canclini, N. 1993. *Transforming Modernity: Popular Culture in Mexico.* Trans. Lidia Lozano. Austin: University of Texas Press.

―――. 1995. *Hybrid Cultures: Strategies for Entering and Leaving Modernity.* Minneapolis: University of Minnesota Press.

―――. 1998. "La ciudad y los medios: Imaginarios del espectáculo y la participación." In N. García Canclini, ed., *Cultura y comunicación en la Ciudad de México* (vol. 2, pp. 19–25). Mexico City: UAM/Grijalbo.

Garrido, J. S. 1974. *Historia de la música popular en México: 1896–1973.* Mexico City: Editorial Extemporaneos.

Geijerstam, C. A. 1976. *Popular Music in Mexico.* Albuquerque: University of New Mexico Press.

Gilroy, P. 1990. "Nationalism, History and Ethnic Absolutism." *History Workshop Journal* 30 (Autumn): 114–20.

González, J. A. 1992. "The Confraternity of (Un)Finishable Emotions: Constructing Mexican Telenovelas." *Studies in Latin American Popular Culture* 11:59–92.

Goodwin, A. 1991. "Popular Music and Postmodern Theory." *Cultural Studies* 5 (2): 174–90.

Goody, J. 1977. *The Domestication of the Savage Mind.* Cambridge: Cambridge University Press.

Gorostiza, J. 1932a. Letter to Salvador Ordoñez, April 29. Expediente 1068, Radio Educación. Depto. de Bellas Artes, Archivo Histórico de la SEP, Mexico City.

―――. 1932b. Untitled report, May 10. Expediente 1068, Radio Educación. Depto. de Bellas Artes, Archivo Histórico de la SEP, Mexico City.

Grandante, W. 1983. "Mexican Popular Music at Mid-century: The Role of José Alfredo Jiménez and the Canción Ranchera." *Studies in Latin American Popular Culture* 2:99–114.

Green, D. 1971. *The Containment of Latin America: A History of the Myths and Realities of the Good Neighbor Policy.* Chicago: Quadrangle.

Gutiérrez, F. F., and J. Reina Schement. 1984. "Spanish International Network: The

Flow of Television from Mexico to the United States." *Communication Research* 11 (2): 241–58.

Haber, S. H. 1989. *Industry and Underdevelopment: The Industrialization of Mexico, 1890-1940*. Stanford: Stanford University Press.

Habermas, J. 1989. *The Structural Transformation of the Public Sphere*. Cambridge: MIT Press.

Haglund, D. G. 1984. *Latin America and the Transformation of U.S. Strategic Thought, 1936-1940*. Albuquerque: University of New Mexico Press.

Hall, S. 1981. "Notes on Deconstructing 'the Popular.' " In R. Samuel, ed., *People's History and Socialist Theory* (pp. 227–40, 378–85). London: Routledge and Kegan.

Hallin, D. C. 1994. "Dos Instituciones un Camino: Television and the State in the 1994 Mexican Election." Paper presented at the Nineteenth Annual Congress of the Latin American Studies Association, Washington, D.C.

Hamilton, N. 1982. *The Limits of State Autonomy: Post-revolutionary Mexico*. Princeton: Princeton University Press.

Hart, J. M. 1987. *Revolutionary Mexico*. Berkeley: University of California Press.

Hawley, E. W. 1974. "Herbert Hoover, the Commerce Secretariat, and the Vision of an 'Associative State,' 1921-1928." *Journal of American History* 61 (1): 116–40.

Hayes, J. E. 1993a. "Early Mexican Radio Broadcasting: Media Imperialism, State Paternalism, or Mexican Nationalism?" *Studies in Latin American Popular Culture* 12:31–55.

———. 1993b. "FDR's First Fireside Chat and the Transformation of American Political Communication: A Study of 20th Century Nationalism." Paper presented at the International Communication Association, Washington, D.C.

———. 1994. "Radio Broadcasting and Nation-Building in Mexico and the United States, 1925-1945." Ph.D. diss., University of California, San Diego.

Hayes, J. E., and C. McSherry. 1997. "Radio." In M. S. Werner, ed., *Encyclopedia of Mexico: History, Society, and Culture* (pp. 1218–26). Chicago: Fitzroy Dearborn.

Haynes, K. A. 1991. "Dependency, Postimperialism, and the Mexican Revolution: An Historiographic Review." *Mexican Studies* 7 (2): 225–51.

Heller, T. 1994. "Introducing Labor Mobility into International Economic Integration Processes." Paper presented at the Center for U.S.-Mexican Studies, University of California, San Diego.

Hobsbawm, E. J. 1990. *Nations and Nationalism since 1780: Programme, Myth, Reality*. Cambridge: Cambridge University Press.

Hobsbawm, E. J., and T. Ranger, eds. 1983. *The Invention of Tradition*. Cambridge: Cambridge University Press.

Horwitz, R. B. 1989. *The Irony of Regulatory Reform*. New York: Oxford University Press.

Isaac, R. 1982. *The Transformation of Virginia, 1740-1790*. Chapel Hill: University of North Carolina Press.

Jablons, M. 1949. "Radio in Mexico." *New York Times*, February 27, p. 11.

Jacobs, H. E. 1951. "Television in Mexico." *New York Times*, April 29, p. 9.

Joseph, G. M., and D. Nugent, eds. 1994a. *Everyday Forms of State Formation: Revolution and the Negotiation of Rule in Modern Mexico*. Durham and London: Duke University Press.

———. 1994b. "Popular Culture and State Formation in Revolutionary Mexico." In G. M. Joseph and D. Nugent, eds., *Everyday Forms of State Formation* (pp. 1-19). Durham and London: Duke University Press.

Josephs, R. 1945a. "The Latinos Tune In, Part I." *The Inter-American*, 17-19.

———. 1945b. "The Latinos Tune In, Part II." *The Inter-American*, 26-28.

Kluckhohn, F. L. 1938. "Cardenas Seeks to Cast Mexico in a New Mold." *New York Times Magazine*, April 10, p. 3.

Knight, A. 1985. "The Mexican Revolution: Bourgois? Nationalist? Or Just a 'Great Rebellion'?" *Bulletin of Latin American Research* 4 (2): 1-37.

———. 1987. *U.S.-Mexican Relations, 1910-1940*. Monograph 28. Center for U.S.-Mexican Studies, University of California at San Diego.

———. 1990. "Cardenismo: Juggernaut or Jalopy?" Paper presented at the Conference of Mexican and North American Historians, San Diego, California.

———. 1994a. "Cardenismo: Juggernaut or Jalopy?" *Journal of Latin American Studies* 26 (1): 73-107.

———. 1994b. "Popular Culture and the Revolutionary State in Mexico, 1910-1940." *Hispanic American Historical Review* 74 (3): 393-444.

———. 1994c. "Weapons and Arches in the Mexican Revolutionary Landscape." In G. M. Joseph and D. Nugent, eds., *Everyday Forms of State Formation* (pp. 24-66). Durham and London: Duke University Press.

———. 1998. "Cardenismo: Myth and Reality." Paper presented at the Latin American Studies Association Twenty-first International Congress, Chicago.

Krause, W. C. 1943. "Mexico, Survey of Radio Programs, July." Central Files, box 346, folder "Mexico." CIAA, RG 229, U.S. National Archives, College Park, Md.

Krauze, E. 1997a. "Introduction: Past, Present, and Future." In *Mexico: Biography of Power* (pp. 1-22). New York: Harper Perennial.

———. 1997b. "Lázaro Cárdenas: The Missionary General." In *Mexico: Biography of Power* (pp. 438-80). New York: Harper Perennial.

———. 1997c. *Mexico: Biography of Power*. New York: Harper Perennial.

Kuhlmann, F., A. Alonso, and A. Mateos. 1989. *Comunicaciones: Pasados y futuros*. Mexico: Fondo de Cultura Económica.

Lacey, K. 1994. "From Plauderie to Propaganda: On Women's Radio in Germany, 1924–1935." *Media, Culture, and Society* 16:589–607.

LaFeber, W. 1987. *The New Empire: An Interpretation of American Expansion 1860–1898*. 1963. Reprint. Ithaca: Cornell University Press.

Leal, J. F. 1986. "The Mexican State, 1915–1973: An Historical Interpretation." In N. Hamilton and T. F. Harding, eds., *Modern Mexico* (pp. 21–42). Beverly Hills: Sage.

Lears, T.J.J. 1981. *No Place of Grace*. New York: Pantheon.

Leyva, J. 1992. *Política educativa y comunicación social: La radio en México, 1940–1946*. Mexico City: UNAM.

Lippman, W. 1965. *Public Opinion*. New York: Free Press.

Lomnitz-Adler, C. 1992. *Exits from the Labyrinth: Culture and Ideology in the Mexican National Space*. Berkeley: University of California Press.

Loyo, E. 1990. "La difusión del Marxismo y los medios de comunicación, 1920–1940." Paper presented at the Meeting of Mexican and North American Historians, San Diego.

———. 1994. "Popular Reactions to the Educational Reforms of Cardenismo." In W. H. Beezley, C. E. Martin, and W. E. French, eds., *Rituals of Rule, Rituals of Resistance* (pp. 247–60). Wilmington, Del.: SR Books.

Luna Arroyo, A. 1934. *La labor educativa de Narciso Bassols*. Mexico City: Editorial Patria.

Malkin, E. 1997. "Showtime for Televisa." *Business Week*, September 1, p. 50.

Malkin, E., and M. Landler. 1994. "Will a Yanqui Partner Make TV Azteca a Player?" *Business Week*, May 30, p. 56.

Martin, E. L. 1935. "Cardenas Talks of Mexico's Broad Plan." *New York Times Magazine*, August 11, p. 3.

Martín-Barbero, J. 1988. "Communication from Culture: The Crisis of the National and the Emergence of the Popular." *Media, Culture, and Society* 10:447–65.

———. 1993a. *Communication, Culture and Hegemony: From Media to Mediations*. London: Sage.

———. 1993b. "Latin America: Cultures in the Communication Media." *Journal of Communication* 43 (2): 18–30.

Mason, F. E. 1938. Memo to Lenox R. Lohr, President, April 9. Department Files, box 93, folder 60. The NBC Collection, Wisconsin State Historical Society, Madison.

McAnany, E. G., and A. C. La Pastina. 1994. "Telenovela Audiences: A Review and Methodological Critique of Latin American Research." *Communication Research* 21 (6): 828–49.

McChesney, R. W. 1990. "The Battle for the U.S. Airwaves, 1928–1935." *Journal of Communication* 40 (Autumn): 29–57.

Mejía Barquera, F. 1989. *La industria de la radio y televisión y la política del estado mexicano (1920–1960)*. Mexico City: Fundación Manuel Buendía.

Mejía Prieto, J. 1972. *Historia de la radio y la televisión en México*. Mexico: Editores Asociados.

Meyer, L. 1977. "Historical Roots of the Authoritarian State in Mexico." In J. L. Reyna and R. S. Weinert, eds., *Authoritarianism in Mexico* (pp. 5–19). Philadelphia: Institute for the Study of Human Issues.

Michaels, A. L. 1970. "The Crisis of Cardenismo." *Latin American Studies* 2 (1): 51–79.

Miller, M. N. 1998. *Red, White, and Green: The Maturing of Mexicanidad, 1940–1946*. El Paso: Texas Western Press.

Milmo, J. 1942. Letter to John Royal, May 12. Royal Papers, box 110, folder "Royal—CIAA, 1942–43." The NBC Collection, Wisconsin State Historical Society, Madison.

Monsiváis, C. 1992. " 'Just over That Hill': Notes on Centralism and Regional Cultures." In E. Van-Young, ed., *Mexico's Regions: Comparative History and Development* (pp. 247–54). San Diego: Center for U.S.-Mexican Studies, University of California at San Diego.

———. 1995. "Mythologies." In P. A. Paranaguá, ed., *Mexican Cinema* (pp. 117–27). London: British Film Institute.

Mora, C. J. 1982. *Mexican Cinema: Reflections of a Society, 1896–1980*. Berkeley: University of California Press.

Moreno Rivas, Y. 1989. *Historia de la música popular mexicana*. 1979. Mexico City: Alianza Editorial Mexicana, Consejo Nacional para la Cultura y las Artes.

Moses, W. J. 1988. *The Golden Age of Black Nationalism, 1850–1925*. 1978. Reprint. New York and Oxford: Oxford University Press.

Mosse, G. L. 1985. *Nationalism and Sexuality: Middle-Class Morality and Sexual Norms in Modern Europe*. Madison: University of Wisconsin Press.

———. 1991. *The Nationalization of the Masses: Political Symbolism and Mass Movements in Germany from the Napoleonic Wars through the Third Reich*. Ithaca: Cornell University Press.

NBC. 1941. Plan of Cooperation, undated. Royal Papers, box 112, folder "Royal Short Wave . . . Contracts, 1941–44." The NBC Collection, Wisconsin State Historical Society, Madison.

New York Times. 1930. "Ortiz Rubio Speaks on Radio to Mexico." *New York Times,* February 27, p. 6.

———. 1937. "1,100 Propagandists in a Mexican Bureau." *New York Times,* September 5, p. 12.

———. 1940. "Camacho Has 6-Year Plan." *New York Times,* February 4, p. 27.

New York Times Magazine. 1946. "Newsboy to President: American Style." *New York Times Magazine,* July 21, p. 2.

Niblo, S. R. 1988. *The Impact of War: Mexico and World War II.* Occasional Paper 10. La Trobe University Institute of Latin American Studies.

Nordenstreng, K., and H. Schiller, eds. 1979. *National Sovereignty and International Communication.* Norwood, N.J.: Ablex.

———. 1993. *Beyond National Sovereignty: International Communication in the 1990's.* Norwood, N.J.: Ablex.

Norris, R. C. 1962. "A History of *La Hora Nacional*: Government Broadcasting via Privately Owned Radio Stations in Mexico." Ph.D. diss., University of Michigan.

Oficina Cultural Radiotelefónica [OCR]. 1933a. "[Quarto] concierto de música popular internacional," segunda parte, March 11. Expediente 20, caja 1313. Oficina Cultural Radiotelefónica, Archivo Histórico de la SEP, Mexico City.

———. 1933b. "Actividades diarias, horario general," March–December. Expediente 33, caja 1315. Oficina Cultural Radiotelefónica, Archivo Histórico de la SEP, Mexico City.

———. 1933c. "Cuatros decadas de música popular mexicana, 1833 a 1870," May 6. Expediente 20, caja 1313. Oficina Cultural Radiotelefónica, Archivo Histórico de la SEP, Mexico City.

———. 1933d. "Hora de música popular internacional," February 18, June 3. Expediente 20, caja 1313. Oficina Cultural Radiotelefónica, Archivo Histórico de la SEP, Mexico City.

———. 1933e. "Nuestra música aborigen actual . . . ," May 28. Expediente 32, caja 1316. Oficina Cultural Radiotelefónica, Archivo Histórico de la SEP, Mexico City.

———. 1933f. "Oficina Cultural Radiotelefónica," undated. Expediente 37, caja 1310. Oficina Cultural Radiotelefónica, Archivo Histórico de la SEP, Mexico City.

———. 1933g. "Programa que será radiado . . . por elementos Tlaxcaltecas," May 26. Expediente 32, caja 1316. Oficina Cultural Radiotelefónica, Archivo Histórico de la SEP, Mexico City.

———. 1933h. "Reportes . . . relativos a los conciertos de música michoacana y araucana," February–March. Expediente 33, caja 1315. Oficina Cultural Radiotelefónica, Archivo Histórico de la SEP, Mexico City.

———. 1933i. "Rumbos nuevos," undated. Expediente 20, caja 1313. Oficina Cultural Radiotelefónica, SEP Archivo Histórico de la SEP, Mexico City.

Ogren, K. J. 1989. *The Jazz Revolution: Twenties America and the Meaning of Jazz.* New York: Oxford University Press.

Oliveira, O. S. 1993. "Brazilian Soaps Outshine Hollywood: Is Cultural Imperialism Fading Out?" In K. Nordenstreng and H. I. Schiller, eds., *Beyond National Sovereignty: International Communication in the 1990's* (pp. 116–31). Norwood, N.J.: Ablex.

O'Malley, I. V. 1986. *The Myth of the Revolution: Hero Cults and the Institutionalization of the Mexican State, 1920-1940.* Westport, Conn.: Greenwood Press.

Ong, W. J. 1995. *Orality and Literacy: The Technologizing of the Word.* 1982. Reprint. London: Routledge.

Ortiz Garza, J. L. 1989. *México en guerra: La historia secreta de los negocios entre empresarios mexicanos de la comunicación, los nazis y E.U.A.* Mexico City: Fascículos Planera.

———. 1997. *Una radio entre dos reinos.* Mexico City: Vergara Editores.

Ortiz H., S. 1960. "Bassols, ejemplo de mexicano." In C. B. de Bassols et al., eds., *Narciso Bassols, en memoria* (pp. 39–45). Mexico City: Editorial.

Pannaralla, G. 1999. "Talk Radio in Mexico." Unpublished course paper, University of Iowa.

Paranaguá, P. A., ed. 1995. *Mexican Cinema.* London: British Film Institute.

Partin, E. M. 1973. "The Life, Educational Ideals, and Work of José Vasconcelos (1882-1959)." Ph.D. diss., University of Pennsylvania.

Peña, M. H. 1985. *The Texas-Mexican Conjunto: History of a Working-Class Music.* Austin: University of Texas Press.

Pérez Montfort, R. 1994. *Estampas de nacionalismo popular mexicano: Ensayos sobre cultural popular y nacionalismo.* Mexico City: CIESAS.

Peters, J. D. 1996. "The Uncanniness of Mass Communication in Interwar Social Thought." *Journal of Communication* 46 (3): 108–23.

Pineda, A., and P. A. Paranaguá. 1995. "Mexico and Its Cinema." In P. A. Paranaguá, ed., *Mexican Cinema* (pp. 15–61). London: British Film Institute.

Pineda Franco, A. 1996. "The Cuban Bolero and Its Transculturation to Mexico: The Case of Agustín Lara." *Studies in Latin American Popular Culture* 15:123–29.

Porritt, P. E. 1983. "Nationalism in Twentieth Century Mexican Music." Master's thesis, University of California, Berkeley.

Poulantzas, N. 1978. *State, Power, Socialism.* Trans. Patrick Camiller. London: NLB.

Quiñones, S. 1996. "AM Talk Radio Explodes in Mexico." *Hispanic* 9 (November): 9.

Ramírez, R. 1933. Letter to Agustín Yáñez, March 22. Expediente 76, caja 1311. Oficina Cultural Radiotelefónica, Archivo Histórico de la SEP, Mexico City.

Ramirez Berg, C. 1992. *Cinema of Solitude.* Austin: University of Texas Press.

Ray, G. 1942. Memo to the Ambassador, July 10. Mexico City Embassy, General Records 1937–49, box 251, 874–76. State Department, RG 84, U.S. National Archives, College Park, Md.

———. 1944. Letter to John Dreier, May 10. Central Files, microfilm M973, roll 559, 812.74/545. State Department, RG 84, U.S. National Archives, College Park, Md.

Reyna, J. L., and R. S. Weinert, eds. 1977. *Authoritarianism in Mexico.* Philadelphia: Institute for the Study of Human Issues.

Riggs, T. J. 1947. Confidential Memo, April 23. Mexico City Embassy, Security-Segregated General Records, 1941–49, box 57, 874. State Department, RG 84, U.S. National Archives, College Park, Md.

Rivera-Perez, L. A. 1998. "Culture, Communication, and Politics." Ph.D. diss., University of Iowa.

Robbins, E. H. 1942. Memo to Wallace N. Harrison, April 15. Miscellaneous Records, box 1459, folder "Content Directives Long Range." CIAA, RG 229, U.S. National Archives, College Park, Md.

Rockefeller Foundation. 1937. Memorandum Relative to a Projected Series of Educational and Cultural Radio-Broadcasts to Latin America, June 21. Folder 3170, Pan American Union Radio, 1936–37, box 266, series 200R, R.F. 1.1. Rockefeller Archive Center, Pocantico Hills, N.Y.

———. 1938. "The Americas on the Air." Grants from the Foundation to the Pan American Union, January. Folder 3171, Pan American Union Radio, 1938–39, box 266, series 200R, R.F. 1.1. Rockefeller Archive Center, Pocantico Hills, N.Y.

Rodriguez, A. 1996. "Objectivity and Ethnicity in the Production of the Noticiero Univisión." *Critical Studies in Mass Communication* 13 (1): 59–81.

Rodríguez Lomelí, L. F. 1933a. "Informe . . . Estado de Hidalgo," April 22. Expediente 76, caja 1311. Oficina Cultural Radiotelefónica, Archivo Histórico de la SEP, Mexico City.

———. 1933b. "Informe . . . Estado de Puebla," March 18. Expediente 76, caja 1311. Oficina Cultural Radiotelefónica, Archivo Histórico de la SEP, Mexico City.

———. 1933c. "Informe . . . Estado de Tlaxcala," March 25. Expediente 76, caja 1311. Oficina Cultural Radiotelefónica, Archivo Histórico de la SEP, Mexico City.

———. 1933d. "Informe . . . Zona de Tlalnepantla, México," April 24. Expediente 76, caja 1311. Oficina Cultural Radiotelefónica, Archivo Histórico de la SEP, Mexico City.

Romo, C. 1990. *La otra radio: Voces debiles, voces de esperanza.* Mexico City: FMBAC and IMER.

Rosenberg, E. S. 1982. *Spreading the American Dream: American Economic and Cultural Expansion, 1890–1945.* New York: Hill and Wang.

Royal, J. 1941. Memo to Frank M. Russell, January 17. Royal Papers, box 112, folder "Royal Short Wave Internat. Div., 1940–43." The NBC Collection, Wisconsin State Historical Society, Madison.

Rubin, J. 1996. "Decentering the Regime: Culture and Regional Politics in Mexico." *Latin American Research Review* 31 (3): 85–125.

———. 1997. *Decentering the Regime: Ethnicity, Radicalism, and Democracy in Juchitán, Mexico.* Durham and London: Duke University Press.

Rubio, O. 1942–43. Letter to Phillip Carlin, undated. Royal Papers, box 111, folder "Royal Mexico—Olalla Rubio." The NBC Collection, Wisconsin State Historical Society, Madison.

Ruíz, R. E. 1980. *The Great Rebellion: Mexico, 1905–1924.* New York: W. W. Norton.

———. 1992. *Triumphs and Tragedy.* New York: W. W. Norton.

Salwen, M. B. 1994. *Radio and Television in Cuba: The Pre-Castro Era.* Ames: Iowa State University Press.

Saragoza, A. 1990. *The Monterrey Elite and the Mexican State, 1880–1940.* 1988. Reprint. Austin: University of Texas Press.

———. 1997. "Television." In M. S. Werner, ed., *Encyclopedia of Mexico: History, Society, and Culture.* Chicago: Fitzroy Dearborn.

Sayre, J. 1941. *An Analysis of the Radiobroadcasting Activities of Federal Agencies.* Vol. 3. Cambridge, Mass.: Radiobroadcasting Research Project.

Scannell, P., ed. 1991. *Broadcast Talk.* London: Sage.

Schwoch, J. 1990. *The American Radio Industry and Its Latin American Activities, 1900–1939.* Urbana and Chicago: University of Illinois Press.

Sinclair, J. 1986. "Dependent Development and Broadcasting: 'The Mexican Formula.'" *Media, Culture, and Society* 8:81–101.

Skidmore, T. E., and P. H. Smith. 1997. "Mexico: The Taming of a Revolution." In *Modern Latin America.* 2d ed. New York: Oxford University Press.

Smith, A. D. 1990. "Nacionalismo e indigenismo: La búsqueda de un pasado auténtico." *Estudios interdisciplinarios de America Latina y el Caribe* 1 (2): 5–17.

Smith, K. W. 1972. "The United States Cultural Crusade in Mexico, 1938–1945." Ph.D. diss., University of California, Berkeley.

Sommer, D. 1991. *Foundational Fictions: The National Romances of Latin America.* Berkeley: University of California Press.

Stevenson, R. 1952. *Music in Mexico: A Historical Survey.* New York: Harper.

Straubhaar, J. D. 1991. "Beyond Media Imperialism: Asymmetrical Interdependence and Cultural Proximity." *Critical Studies in Mass Communication* 8 (March): 39–59.

Susman, W. I. 1984. *Culture as History: The Transformation of American Society in the Twentieth Century.* New York: Pantheon.

Suvanandan, A. 1998–99. "Globalism and the Left." *Race and Class* 40 (2–3): 5–19.

Sydney Ross 1942. Radio Survey, Mexico City, June 27–August 13. Central Files, box 346. CIAA, RG 229, U.S. National Archives, College Park, Md.

Thornburn, D. 1947. World Advtg.—on Mexico. *Tide, the Magazine for Advertising Executives,* July 11, 26–31.

Tomlinson, J. 1992. *Cultural Imperialism.* Baltimore: Johns Hopkins University Press.

Torres Ramírez, B. 1979. *México en la Segunda Guerra Mundial.* Mexico City: El Colegio de México.

Townsend, W. C. 1952. *Lazaro Cardenas: Mexican Democrat.* Ann Arbor: George Wahr.

Trigo, A. 1996. "On Transculturation: Toward a Political Economy of Culture in the Periphery." *Studies in Latin American Popular Culture* 15:99–117.

U.S. State Department. 1944. Telegram from State Department to Mexico City Embassy, March 6. General Records 1937–49, box 529, 872–877K. State Department, RG 84, U.S. National Archives, College Park, Md.

Van Young, E., ed. 1992. *Mexico's Regions: Comparative History and Development.* San Diego: Center for U.S.-Mexican Studies, Univ. of California at San Diego.

———. 1994. "Conclusion: The State as Vampire—Hegemonic Projects, Public Rituals, and Popular Culture in Mexico, 1600–1900." In W. H. Beezley, C. E. Martin, and W. E. French, eds., *Rituals of Rule, Rituals of Resistance* (pp. 343–74). Wilmington, Del.: SR Books.

Vaughan, M. K. 1982. *The State, Education, and Social Class in Mexico, 1880–1920.* De Kalb: Northern Illinois University Press.

———. 1997. *Cultural Politics in Revolution: Teachers, Peasants, and Schools in Mexico, 1930–1940.* Tucson: University of Arizona Press.

———. 1999. "Cultural Approaches to Peasant Politics in the Mexican Revolution." *Hispanic American Historical Review* 79 (2): 269–305.

Vaughan, M. K., and S. E. Lewis, eds. n.d. *Forging a Nation: Mexico's Cultural Revolution, 1920–1940.* Forthcoming from Duke University Press.

Vázquez, J. Z., and L. Meyer. 1985. *The United States and Mexico*. Chicago: University of Chicago Press.

Vázquez Valle, I., ed. 1989. *La cultura popular vista por las elites*. Mexico City: UNAM.

Vogel, G. J. 1943. Memo to John Ogilvie, May 4. Central Files, box 292, folder "Reports, March 1, 1943." CIAA, RG 229, U.S. National Archives, College Park, Md.

Westbrook, R. B. 1990. " 'I Want a Girl, Just Like the Girl That Married Harry James': American Women and the Problem of Political Obligation in World War II." *American Quarterly* 42 (4): 587–614.

Weyl, N., and S. Weyl. 1939. *The Reconquest of Mexico*. London: Oxford University Press.

White, E. F. 1990. "Africa on My Mind: Gender, Counter Discourse and African-American Nationalism." *Journal of Women's History* 2 (1): 73–97.

Wilkie, J. W., and C. A. Contreras, eds. 1992. *Statistical Abstract of Latin America*. Vol. 29, pt. 1. Los Angeles: UCLA Latin American Center Publications.

Williams, J. 1942. Memo to Fred Bate, December 12. Royal Papers, box 111, folder "Royal Mexico, Spanish News for Mexico, 1942–43." The NBC Collection, Wisconsin State Historical Society, Madison.

Williams, R. 1973. *The County and the City*. New York: Oxford University Press.

———. 1974. *Television: Technology and Cultural Form*. New York: Schocken Books.

———. 1977. *Marxism and Literature*. Oxford: Oxford University Press.

Winner, P. 1938. Work in Progress. Undated memo. Department Files, box 93, folder 61. The NBC Collection, Wisconsin State Historical Society, Madison.

Winocur, R. 1998. "Radio y ciudadanos: Usos privados de una voz pública." In N. García Canclini, ed., *Cultura y comunicación en la Ciudad de México* (vol. 2, pp. 127–55). Mexico City: UAM/Grijalbo.

Yáñez, A. 1932. "Ideas para la reorganización . . .," Feb 28. Expediente 1068, Radio Educación. Depto. de Bellas Artes, Archivo Histórico de la SEP, Mexico City.

———. 1933a. Letter to Director de Educación Federal, Edo. de Jalisco, May 31. Expediente 32, caja 1316. Oficina Cultural Radiotelefónica, Archivo Histórico de la SEP, Mexico City.

———. 1933b. Letter to Rafael Ramírez, March 27. Expediente 76, caja 1311. Oficina Cultural Radiotelefónica, Archivo Histórico de la SEP, Mexico City.

Zamba, M. J. 1996. "Mexico: Media Metamorphosis." *Masthead* 48 (Fall): 72–73.

Index

About the Author

Joy Elizabeth Hayes is currently Assistant Professor of Communication Studies at the University of Iowa. She holds an M.A. in history and a Ph.D. in communication from the University of California, San Diego. Her research interests include the cultural history of broadcasting in the Americas, mass media audiences in historical perspective, and the historical role of communication media in nation formation. Her articles on Mexican broadcasting have been published in the *Communication Review* and *Studies in Latin American Popular Culture*.